Contents

Age-Appropriate Skills

Language

- following directions
- story comprehension
- descriptive and comparative language
- rhyming
- categorization
- letter and sound recognition
- statements and questions
- auditory and visual memory
- left to right tracking
- oral language
- vocabulary and concept development
- sequencing
- color words

Math

- counting to 20
- patterning
- numeral recognition
- geometric shapes
- ordinal numbers
- beginning computation
- one-to-one matching
- graphing
- measurement

Contents

Making Circle-Time Books ....

Follow these simple directions to assemble a circle-time book for each of the five sections of *Insects*.

- Tear out and laminate the color story pages for each circle-time book.

- Bind the books with binder rings or an alternative binding method.

- Read the circle-time book as the opening activity for each section of *Insects*.

Place the book on an easel or chalkboard stand and flip the pages for easy reading.

Sharing Circle-Time Books ....

Each circle-time story introduces the topic of that section. Begin by reading the story to the children several times. The first time you read it, you might ask children to predict what the story will be about by looking at the cover illustration. In subsequent readings, use strategies such as:

- moving your finger under words as you read to model left to right tracking

- allowing children to "read" the predictable text

- asking children to identify objects in the pictures

- talking about any rhyming words

- asking children to predict what will happen next in the story

- asking questions to help children recall story details

- asking at least one question that relates to children's own lives

Circle-Time Books

What Is an Insect?

"Bug Jars" (pages 13–22)
Use this colorful book to introduce children to the insect unit. Pause on each page and discuss the illustrations. Allow children to share what they know about the insect shown. Explain that they will be learning all about different kinds of insects, their body parts, how they grow, and also about insects that are helpful to people.

Ask questions such as:
- What insect does Linda have in her jar?
- Why do you think the children in the story caught insects?
- What do you think they will do with the insects?
- Can you name the parts of an insect?
- What insects have you seen outside?

Section Two
About Insects

"Insects" (pages 51–60)
This book introduces children to the differences in insects. It covers their different homes and how various insects move, eat, and lay eggs.

Ask questions such as:
- How can insects move?
- How does a butterfly eat?
- What kind of home does a bee have?
- How are a ladybug and a grasshopper alike? How are they different?
- How are you like an insect? How are you different?

Section Three
Insect Life Cycles

"Egg, Caterpillar, Butterfly" (pages 91–100)
This sequential story shows the life cycle of the butterfly from egg to adult. As you read the story, have children look carefully at the illustrations to see the changes that are occurring. Discuss changes they have seen in their own pets and in themselves as they grow. Explain the meaning of *caterpillar*, *chrysalis*, and *jade*.

Ask questions such as:
- What happened to the egg?
- How did the caterpillar change?
- What happened inside the chrysalis?
- How have you changed since you were a baby?

Note: Consider raising butterflies in the classroom. It is an exciting way for students to experience the cycle of life. Check science supply catalogs for sources of butterfly kits. Or check your own neighborhood for eggs you can hatch.

Circle-Time Books

"Good Bugs!" (pages 125–134)
This story shows children some of the ways in which insects are helpful. Pause on each page and discuss the illustrations. If possible, provide silk thread, silk cloth, and honey for children to experience after hearing the story.

Ask questions such as:

- How are ladybugs helpful?
- What do we get from a silkworm moth caterpillar?
- What do bees make that we can use?
- Have you ever eaten honey? Do you like it?

"What Is It?" (pages 161–170)
This story helps children recognize the differences between an insect and a spider. Guide children to understand that catching and eating insects makes a spider a helpful creature.

Ask questions such as:

- Which has more legs, a spider or an insect? How many more?
- What are some other ways an insect and a spider are different?
- Why does a spider spin a web?
- Have you seen a real spider or a web? Tell about it.

Take-Home Books

Use these simple directions to make reproducible take-home books for each of the five sections of *Insects*.

1. Reproduce the book pages for each child.
2. Cut the pages along the cut lines.
3. Place the pages in order, or this may be done as a sequencing activity with children. Guide children in assembling the book page by page.
4. Staple the book together.

After making each take-home book, review the story as children turn the pages of their own books. Send the storybook home along with the Parent Letter on page 5.

Dear Parent(s) or Guardian(s),

As part of our unit *Insects*, I will be presenting five storybooks to the class. Your child will receive a take-home storybook for you to share. Remember that reading to children helps them develop a love of reading. Regularly reading aloud to children has proven to enhance a variety of early language skills, including:

- vocabulary and concept development,
- letter recognition,
- phonemic awareness,
- auditory and visual discrimination, and
- left to right tracking.

I hope you enjoy sharing these stories with your child.

As you read to your child, remember to:

1. speak clearly and with interest.
2. track words by moving your finger under each word as you read it.
3. ask your child to help you identify objects in the pictures. Talk about these objects together.
4. discuss your own experiences as they relate to the story.
5. allow your child to express his or her own thoughts and ideas and to ask you questions.

I hope you enjoy all five of these stories.

Sincerely,

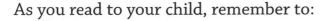

Storyboards

A storyboard is an excellent way to enhance vocabulary and concept development.

Each section of *Insects* includes full-color storyboard pieces to use in extending the language and concepts introduced. Ideas for using the storyboard pieces in each section are found on pages 7–9.

Turn the full-color cutouts into pieces that will adhere to a flannel- or felt-covered storyboard. Just laminate the pieces and affix self-sticking Velcro® dots to the back of each piece.

What Is an Insect?
pages 29 and 31

About Insects
pages 67 and 69

Insect Life Cycles
pages 107 and 109

Insect Helpers
pages 141 and 143

A Spider Is Not an Insect!
pages 177 and 179

Storyboards

"Bug Jars" Storyboard Use the colorful storyboard pieces on pages 29 and 31 to follow up your presentation of the story "Bug Jars." You may choose to use the following teacher script to present the story:

(Place Linda, Manuel, and Greg on the storyboard.)
Here are the children from our story. (Point to the children one at a time.)
Who can tell me his/her name? (Place the bug jars along the edge of the storyboard. Point to the jars one at a time.) *What is in this jar? Who caught the* (name the insect)? (Place the jar next to the correct person.)

When all of the children and insects have been named and matched, remove the storyboard pieces and allow children to replace each piece as they tell about it.

Next, put the ladybug on the storyboard. Ask children:
How many legs does the ladybug have? (6)
How many body parts does the ladybug have? (3)
How many antennae does the ladybug have? (2)
What kind of animal is a ladybug? (insect)

Remove the storyboard pieces and allow children to replace each piece as they retell the story.

"Insects" Storyboard Use the colorful storyboard pieces on pages 67 and 69 to follow up your presentation of the story "Insects." You may choose to use the following teacher script to present the story:

Place the insects on the storyboard.
Point to each insect as you talk about what it is doing.

- *These insects are eating. The ladybug is chewing on an aphid. The butterfly is sipping nectar from the flower. The grasshopper is eating a leaf.*

- *These insects are laying eggs. The ladybug is laying eggs on a leaf. The grasshopper is laying eggs in the ground. The ants lay their eggs underground, too.*

- *These insects are moving. The grasshopper is hopping. The water bug is swimming. The dragonfly is flying.*

Remove the storyboard pieces and allow children to replace each piece as they retell the story.

Storyboards

"Egg, Caterpillar, Butterfly" Storyboard Use the colorful storyboard pieces on pages 107 and 109 to follow up your presentation of the story "Egg, Caterpillar, Butterfly." You may choose to use the following teacher script to present the story:

Scatter the pictures around the storyboard, leaving an area at the top of the board for arranging the pictures in sequence. *Today we are going to talk about how a butterfly grows.*

- *These are eggs and little caterpillars.*
- *This is a caterpillar that has grown bigger.*
- *Now it has grown even bigger.*
- *The caterpillar is in this chrysalis.*
- *Now it is a butterfly, drying its wings.*
- *The change is complete. The caterpillar is a butterfly.*

Now let's put the pictures in order. Let's start with the eggs. What will hatch out of the eggs? That's right. Little caterpillars hatch from the eggs. Place the small caterpillar after the eggs. Continue with each of the stages, naming the item and placing it in the correct order. *Let's name each part one more time.* Point and name each stage again.

Remove the storyboard pieces and allow children to replace each piece as they retell the story.

"Insect Helpers" Storyboard Use the colorful storyboard pieces on pages 141 and 143 to follow up your presentation of the story "Good Bugs!" You may choose to use the following teacher script to present the story:

Another name for a bug is "insect." Some insects eat our plants or carry diseases. But there are also good insects. Let's use our storyboard pieces to talk about some good insects and how they help us. As you talk, match the good insect to what it can do.

- *There are aphids on this leaf. The aphids are eating the leaf. This is not good for the plant. But there is a good insect that can help. This ladybug will eat the aphids.*
- *This is silk thread. The silk comes from a special caterpillar. It is the caterpillar of the silkworm moth.*

As you talk about the honeybee, place each item on the storyboard. *When the honeybee lands on a plant, it picks up a yellow powder on its legs. Can you see this on the honeybee's legs?*

- *This powder is called pollen. When the honeybee lands on the next flower, it leaves some pollen. This helps new plants to grow.*
- *The honeybee sips sweet juice, or nectar, from the flower. The bee takes the pollen and the nectar back to the beehive. Honeybees make honey. The honey is put into the parts of the honeycomb in the beehive. Bees use the honey for food. We can eat the honey, too.*

Remove the storyboard pieces and allow children to replace each piece as they retell the story.

Section Five
A Spider Is Not an Insect!

"What Is It?" Storyboard Use the colorful storyboard pieces on pages 177 and 179 to follow up your presentation of the story "What Is It?" Children categorize insects and spiders using the number of legs as a clue. You may choose to use the following teacher script to present the story:

What did the girl in the story see? That's right. She saw a spider.
Place the spider and the ladybug on the storyboard. Who can show me the spider? How do you know that it is a spider? Yes, it has eight legs. Let's count them. How many legs does the insect have? Let's count them. Have any of you ever seen a spider? How did you know it was a spider? What was the spider doing?

Place the remaining pictures on the storyboard. Ask children to identify each picture and then explain how they know if it is a spider or an insect.

Remove the storyboard pieces and allow children to replace each piece as they retell the story.

Creating an Atmosphere

Turn your classroom into a delightful nature environment overflowing with information about insects. Use a large basket to hold books about insects for children to share.

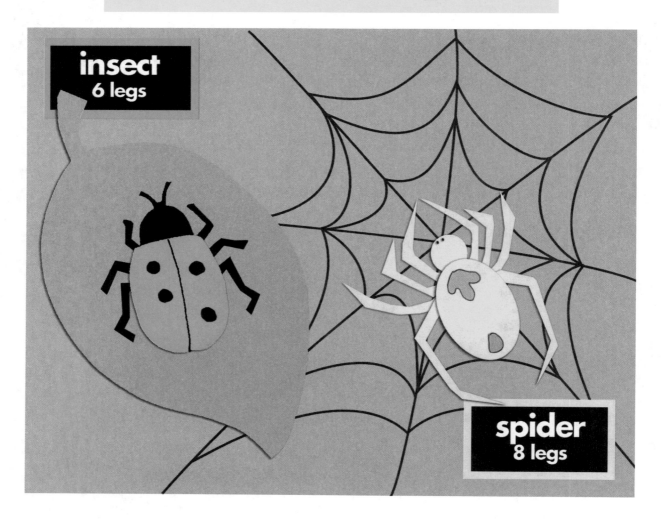

How Many Legs?

insect
6 legs

spider
8 legs

Make a Bulletin Board About Insects

• Staple blue butcher paper to the board as a backing.
• Draw a giant web with a black marker on one side of the board.

Simple Steps to Show You How

Leaf
- Cut out a giant leaf from green butcher or construction paper.
- Staple it next to the web on the blue paper.

Insect
- Make a ladybug to represent the insect family. Use red and black paper to cut the shapes as shown. Add details with a marker.

Spider
- Cut a large spider from yellow paper. Add details with a marker. Pin it to the board.

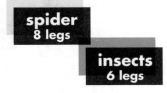

Labels
- Cut out backing and letters to label the insect and the spider.

Title
- Cut out letters for the title—**How Many Legs?**
- Attach the letters to a strip of yellow paper and staple it to the board.

What Is an Insect?

Children are introduced to insects.
They will learn to identify and name some common
insects and the characteristics of all insects.

Note: Teachers will make copies
and cut in half for minibooks.

Reproducible Story

Bug
Jars

Linda has ladybugs
in her bug jar.

1

Note: Teachers will make copies and cut in half for minibooks.

A ladybug has

   6 legs,

   3 body parts, and

   2 antennae.

2

Manuel has

a moth in his

bug jar.

3

A moth has

6 legs,

3 body parts, and

2 antennae.

4

Greg has

a grasshopper

in his bug jar.

5

Note: Teachers will make copies and cut in half for minibooks.

A grasshopper has
6 legs,
3 body parts, and
2 antennae.

6

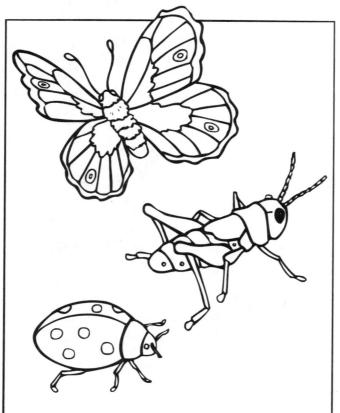

A ladybug, a moth,
and a grasshopper
are all insects.

7

Note: Teachers will make copies and cut in half for minibooks.

Reproducible Story

And all insects have
6 legs,
3 body parts, and
2 antennae.

8

The End

Note: Children cut out the insects and glue them in the correct jar. Then they draw an insect in the last jar.

Name _____

In the Bug Jars

Color. Cut. Glue.

Draw.

Note: See page 7 for suggestions on using the storyboard pieces on pages 29 and 31 for Bug Jars.

Storyboard Pieces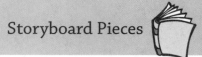

What Is an Insect?

©2005 by Evan-Moor Corp.
All About Insects • EMC 2405

What Is
an Insect?

©2005 by Evan-Moor Corp.
All About Insects
EMC 2405

What Is
an Insect?

©2005 by Evan-Moor Corp.
All About Insects
EMC 2405

What Is
an Insect?

©2005 by Evan-Moor Corp.
All About Insects
EMC 2405

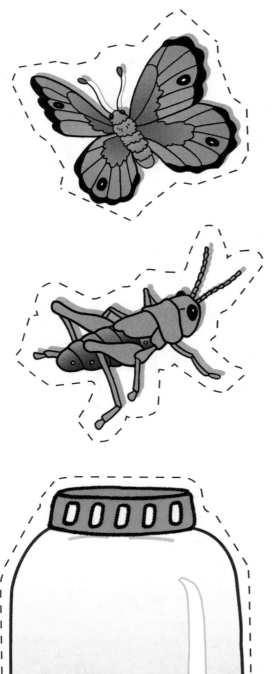

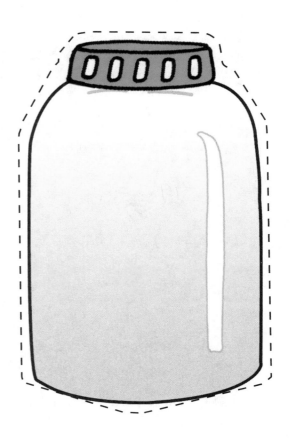

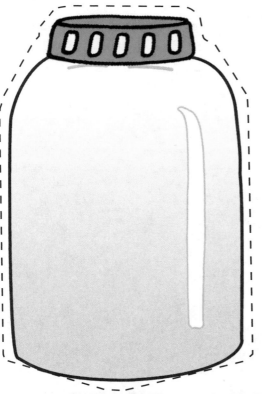

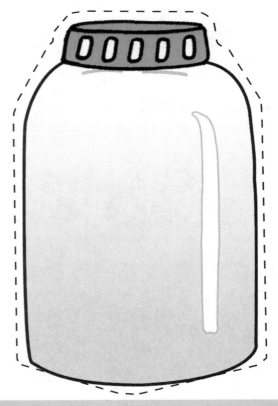

What Is an Insect?   **31**

What Is an Insect?

What Is an Insect?

What Is an Insect?

What Is an Insect?

What Is an Insect?

Children create their own insects from baker's clay and pipe cleaners.

Materials

- 1 cup (188 g) salt
- 1½ cups (360 mL) hot water
- 5 cups (625 g) flour
- optional: food coloring
- pipe cleaners or broom straws (cut into short pieces)
- pencil
- baking sheet
- access to an oven
- water
- small paper cups

Baker's Clay Bugs

Steps to Follow

1. Give each child a lump of baker's clay and a paper cup containing a small amount of water.
2. Children form their insects from the clay. Using a sharpened pencil, they make eyes and a mouth.
3. Then children use pipe-cleaner or broom-straw pieces for antennae and legs.
4. Place the finished insects on a baking sheet. Write each child's name on the underside of his or her insect.
5. Bake the insects at 300°F (150°C) until hard. Cool.

Baker's Clay

1. Dissolve the salt in hot water. Optional: Add a few drops of food coloring.
2. Stir in the flour.
3. Knead the dough until pliable (about 5 minutes).
4. Store in an airtight container.

Extension

Color the baked insects with markers and then spray with clear acrylic glaze.

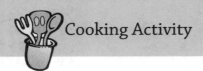
Cooking Activity

Ladybug Cookies

Make these yummy ladybugs to munch on at snack time.

Steps to Follow

1. Using a dull plastic knife, children spread red frosting onto a cookie. They place the cookie on a paper plate.

2. Then they place the black candy "head" on the cookie.

3. Using the knife, children start at the head and draw a line down the middle of the cookie.

4. Then they place three chocolate chips on each side of the line.

5. Children add three small strips of licorice whips or pretzel sticks on each side of the ladybug for legs, and then add two on the head for antennae.

Extension

As children eat their ladybug cookies, review the parts of an insect. Discuss which parts they made on their cookies and which parts are missing.

Materials

- plain round sugar cookies
- red frosting
- black mini-gumdrops or black Dots® candy (for heads)
- chocolate chips (for spots)
- dull plastic knives
- paper plates
- hand wipes
- paper towels
- small strips of licorice whips or pieces of pretzel sticks (for antennae and legs)

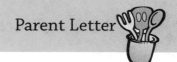

Dear Parent(s) or Guardian(s),

Today we cooked in class. Your child made "Ladybug Cookies." Besides having fun cooking and eating, the children practiced these skills:

- listening to and following directions
- vocabulary development
- using small motor skills

For our unit *Insects*, we will send home a variety of new recipes. Each recipe will be one that your child has tried in class and is excited about. We hope you have an opportunity to try this recipe again with your child. Allowing your child to help you in the kitchen is a wonderful way to reinforce learning skills while creating family memories.

Ladybug Cookies

Materials

- plain round sugar cookies
- red frosting
- black mini-gumdrops or black Dots® candy (for heads)
- chocolate chips (for spots)
- dull plastic knife
- paper plates
- hand wipes
- paper towels
- small strips of licorice whips or pretzel sticks (for antennae and legs)

Steps to Follow

1. Prepare a work area with tools and ingredients.
2. Frost a sugar cookie with red frosting.
3. Attach a black candy head to the cookie. Using a dull plastic knife, draw a line down the middle of the cookie, starting at the head.
4. Finally, place three chocolate chips on each side of the line.
5. Add three small strips of licorice whips or pretzel sticks on each side of the ladybug for legs.
6. Enjoy your ladybug cookies!

Name _____

Ladybug, Ladybug

Color the pictures that begin like **ladybug**.

Note: Review color words with children. Then lead the class in correctly coloring the insects below.

Language—Word Recognition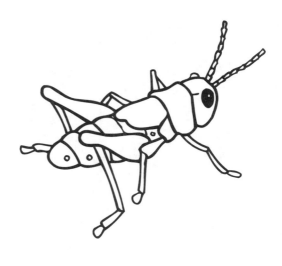

Name _____

Colorful Insects

Color the insects.

red

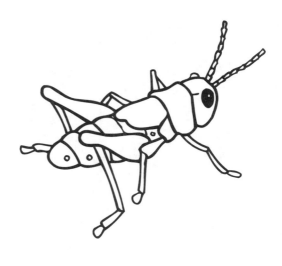

green

yellow

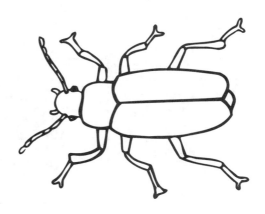

black

Note: Children cut out and glue the pictures to complete each pattern.

Name _____

Complete the Patterns

Cut. Glue.

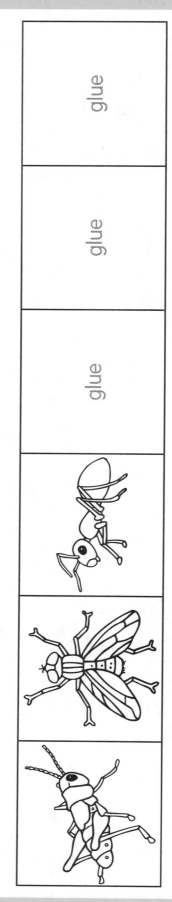

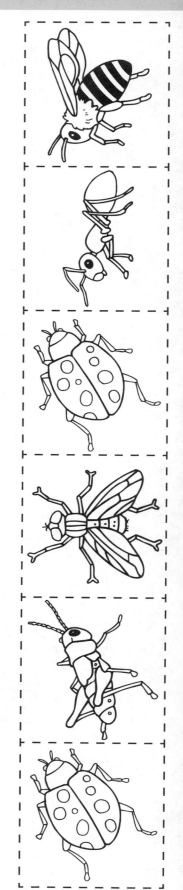

All About Insects • EMC 2405 • ©2005 by Evan-Moor Corp.

Note: Children count the number of ladybugs in each jar, and then write the number in the box.

How Many Ladybugs?

Name _____

Count. Write.

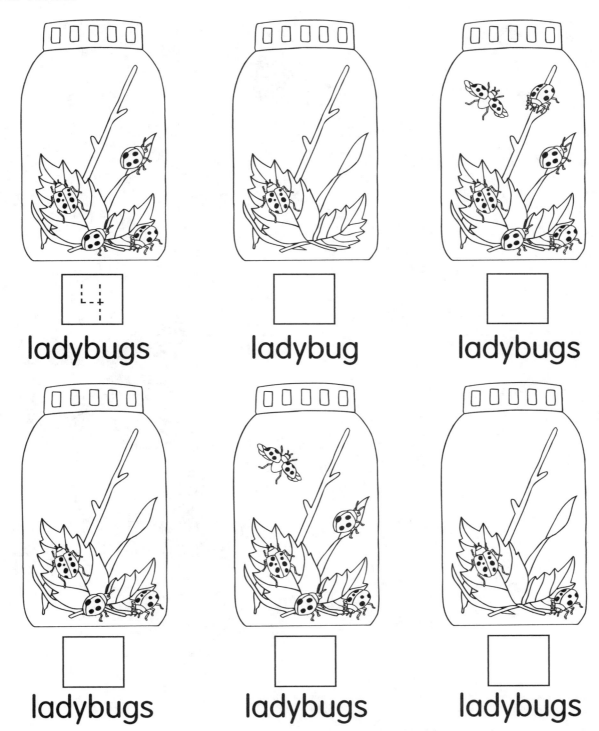

4

ladybugs

ladybug

ladybugs

ladybugs

ladybugs

ladybugs

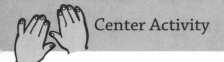

Working independently or in pairs, children put together insect puzzles.

Insect Puzzles

Creating the Center

1. Laminate and cut apart pages 41–45.

2. Place each puzzle in its own envelope. Glue the name label provided to the outside of each envelope.

3. Place the puzzle envelopes in a sturdy folder or larger envelope.

4. Plan time to model how the center is used.

Using the Center

1. Children may use the center individually or with a partner.

2. Children put together one or more of the insect puzzles.

Materials

- pages 41–45, laminated
- envelopes
- scissors
- glue
- sturdy folder or large envelope

ladybug

What Is an Insect?

©2005 by Evan-Moor Corp.
All About Insects • EMC 2405

What Is an Insect?

©2005 by Evan-Moor Corp.
All About Insects • EMC 2405

What Is an Insect?

©2005 by Evan-Moor Corp.
All About Insects • EMC 2405

What Is an Insect?

©2005 by Evan-Moor Corp.
All About Insects • EMC 2405

What Is an Insect?

©2005 by Evan-Moor Corp. • All About Insects • EMC 2405

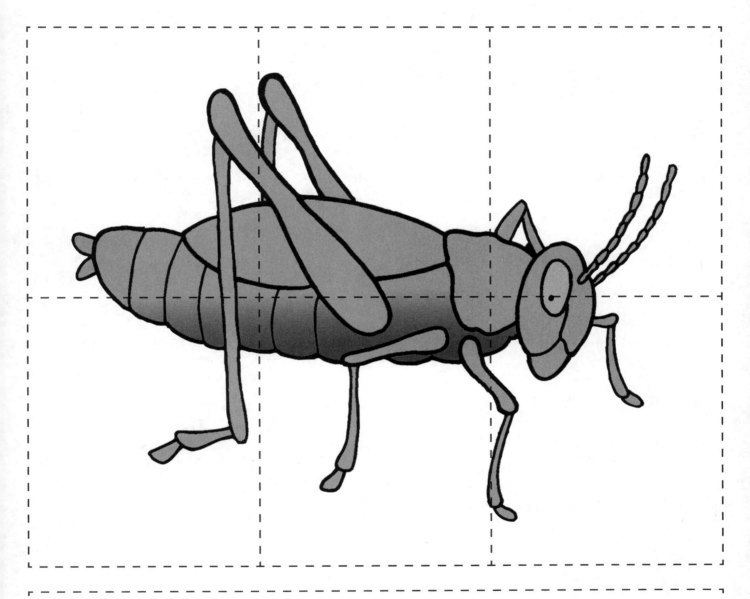

grasshopper

What Is an Insect?

What Is an Insect?

What Is an Insect?

What Is an Insect?

What Is an Insect?

What Is an Insect?

What Is an Insect?

moth

What Is an Insect?

©2005 by Evan-Moor Corp.
All About Insects • EMC 2405

What Is an Insect?

©2005 by Evan-Moor Corp.
All About Insects • EMC 2405

What Is an Insect?

©2005 by Evan-Moor Corp.
All About Insects • EMC 2405

What Is an Insect?

©2005 by Evan-Moor Corp.
All About Insects • EMC 2405

What Is an Insect?

©2005 by Evan-Moor Corp. • All About Insects • EMC 2405

Note: Bugs in Jars is a variation of the game Squirrels in Trees.

Outdoor Activity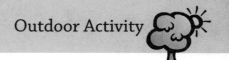

Children try to catch a "bug" in their "jar."

Bugs in Jars

How to Play

1. Children line up in an outdoor space. Tap each child and label him or her "jar," "jar," "bug." Continue until you have 1 or 2 children left and label them "bugs."

2. Have each pair of jars hold hands to form a jar.

3. Have a bug enclosed in each jar (except the extra bugs). There should be jars and bugs scattered all over the play area.

4. Blow a whistle or yell *Go!* The bugs will then leave the jar they are in and run to a new jar. One or two bugs will be left outside a jar each time. They will continue to try to get into a jar each time the whistle blows.

5. Play continues until time has run out.

bug jar

bug

Note: Select a group of children to be the five little insects. Have them act out each verse as it is repeated.

Five Little Insects

5 little insects
sitting on the floor,
1 hopped away
and then there were 4.

4 little insects
sitting in a tree,
1 flew away
and then there were 3.

3 little insects
sitting on my shoe,
1 crawled away
and then there were 2.

2 little insects
sitting on a bun,
1 ran away
and then there was 1.

1 little insect
having lots of fun,
it flew away home
and then there were none.

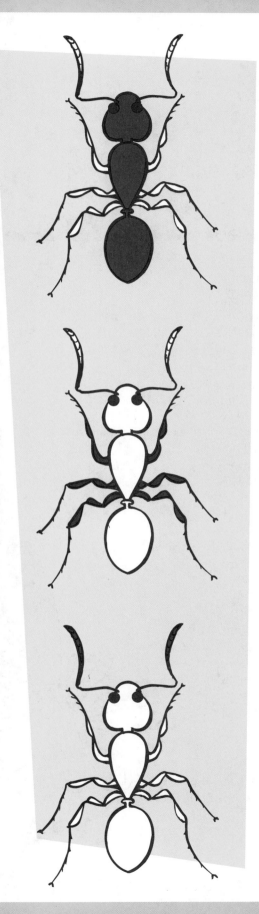

Every Insect

Every insect has three parts,
    has three parts,
    has three parts.
Every insect has three parts,
Each ant and moth and bee.

Every insect has six legs,
    has six legs,
    has six legs.
Every insect has six legs,
Each ant and moth and bee.

Every insect has two antennae,
    has two antennae,
    has two antennae.
Every insect has two antennae,
Each ant and moth and bee.

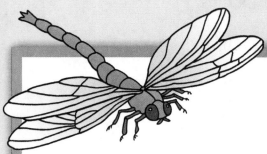

About Insects

Children are introduced to some of the behaviors of insects.

Note: Teachers will make copies and cut in half for minibooks.

Reproducible Story

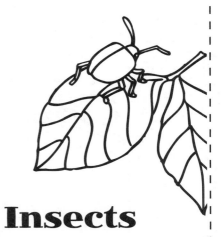

Insects

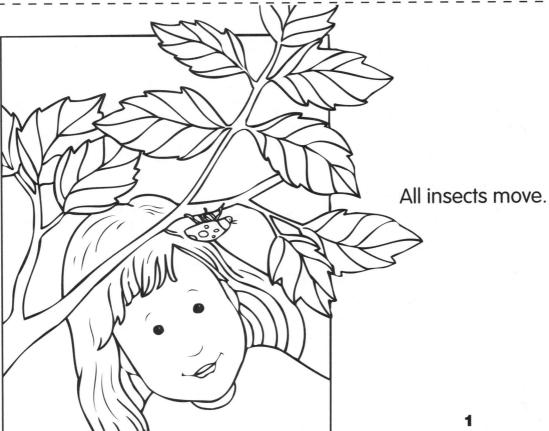

All insects move.

1

Reproducible Story

Note: Teachers will make copies and cut in half for minibooks.

But not all insects move

in the same way.

Some fly.

Some hop.

Some swim.

2

All insects eat food.

3

But not all insects
eat the same food.
Some sip.
Some chew.

4

All insects lay eggs.

5

Reproducible Story

Note: Teachers will make copies and cut in half for minibooks.

But not all eggs are
the same.

6

Insects live in
many places.

7

Note: Teachers will make copies and cut in half for minibooks.

Reproducible Story

But not all insects live in the same place.

8

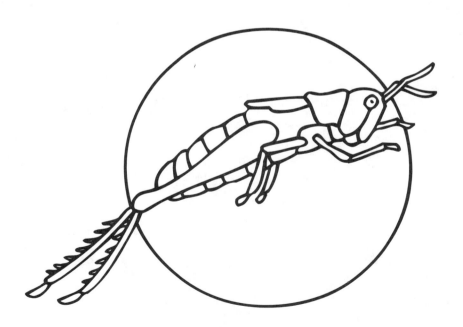

The End

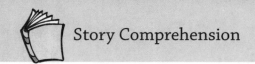

Note: Review the insect homes shown in the story Insects. Children draw a line from each insect to its home.

Name _____

Where Do I Live?

Draw a line.

Make a match.

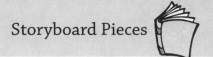

Note: See page 7 for suggestions on using the storyboard pieces on pages 67 and 69 for Insects.

About Insects

About Insects

About Insects

About Insects

About Insects

©2005 by Evan-Moor Corp.
All About Insects • EMC 2405

About Insects

©2005 by Evan-Moor Corp.
All About Insects • EMC 2405

About Insects

©2005 by Evan-Moor Corp.
All About Insects • EMC 2405

About Insects

©2005 by Evan-Moor Corp.
All About Insects • EMC 2405

About Insects

©2005 by Evan-Moor Corp.
All About Insects • EMC 2405

Children create gigantic insects using tempera paints.

Materials

- cards on pages 79–83
- large paint paper
- tempera paint in various colors
- paintbrushes
- paint smocks or aprons

Let's Paint BIG Insects

Preparation

Using the picture cards on pages 79, 81, and 83, review with children the various kinds of insects. Talk about the body parts, colors, and designs of each insect.

Steps to Follow

1. Children choose one insect to paint. Remind children to paint the insect large enough to fill the page.

2. After completing their painting, children count their insect's body parts to make sure each has 3 body parts, 6 legs, and 2 antennae.

Extension

Cover a large bulletin board with butcher paper. Cut out the completed insects and pin them to the board for everyone to see. Add labels to each insect, naming the type of insect and the painter.

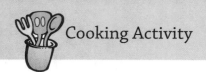
Note: Check for allergies before beginning any cooking activity. An allergic reaction can occur through taste, smell, or contact with allergens.

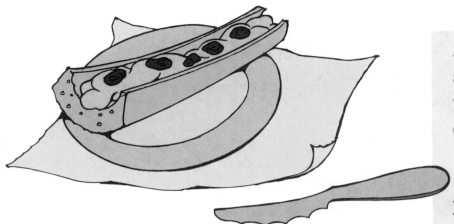

Ants on a log were never so yummy! Children will enjoy making these delicious treats.

Five Ants on a Log

Steps to Follow

1. Children place a celery stalk on a paper plate.
2. They take a spoonful of cheese and place it on the celery stalk. Children use a dull plastic knife to spread the cheese onto the celery stalk.
3. Then children place a row of five raisin "ants" on top of the cheese.
4. Children enjoy their tasty treat.

Extensions

1. Ask children to think of other things that could be stuffed into their celery to make a yummy snack.
2. Share your favorite ant book with the children.

Materials

- celery stalks, one per child
- soft cheese (fruit-flavored cream cheese, Cheez Whiz®, etc.)
- raisins
- small paper plates, one per child
- dull plastic knives and spoons
- napkins

Dear Parent(s) or Guardian(s),

Today we cooked in class. Your child made a snack called "Five Ants on a Log." Besides having fun cooking and eating, the children practiced these skills:

- listening to and following directions
- vocabulary development
- using small motor skills

For our unit *Insects*, we will send home a variety of new recipes. Each recipe will be one that your child has tried in class and is excited about. We hope you have an opportunity to try this recipe again with your child. Allowing your child to help you in the kitchen is a wonderful way to reinforce learning skills while creating family memories.

Five Ants on a Log

Materials

- celery stalks, cleaned
- soft cheese (fruit-flavored cream cheese, Cheez Whiz®, etc.)
- raisins
- small plates
- plastic knives and spoons
- paper towels for cleanup

Steps to Follow

1. Spoon cheese onto each celery stalk and then spread it along the stalk.
2. Then place a row of raisin "ants" on top of the cheese.
3. Enjoy this healthy snack!

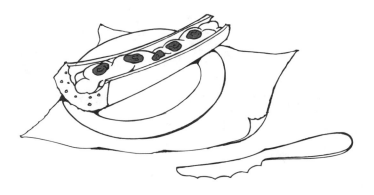

ABC Language—Auditory Discrimination

Note: Children say the name of each picture. Then they color the pictures whose names begin with the /b/ sound.

Name _____

Listen for the Sound

Bb

bee

Color the pictures that begin like **bee**.

Note: Read the directions to the children. Explain that the ant is carrying food to the anthill. Children help by coloring a path for the hardworking ant.

Language—Word Recognition ABC

Name _____

Busy Ant

Help the ant get to the anthill.

Color the boxes with the word **ant**.

ant	ant	fly	bee	moth
bee	ant	moth	wasp	fly
fly	ant	ant	bee	bee
moth	bee	ant	ant	ant
bee	fly	wasp	bee	ant
wasp	bee	moth	fly	ant

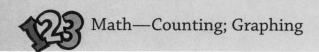

Note: Use the information to guide children through the steps for making a graph.

Name _____

How Many Do You See?

Count. Color a box for each insect.

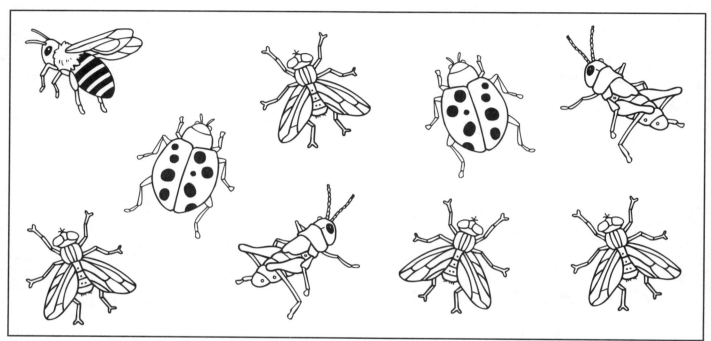

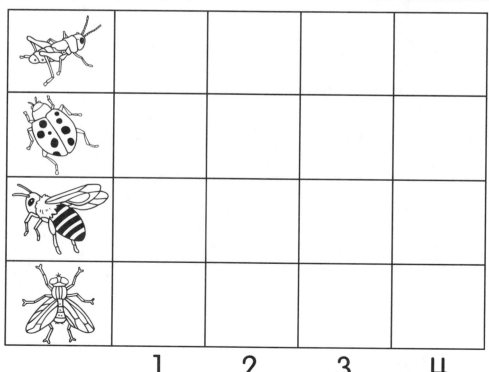

Note: Review the two geometric shapes below with children. Guide children in completing the color key. Children refer to the color key to color the insects.

Name _____

Color the Shapes

 green    red

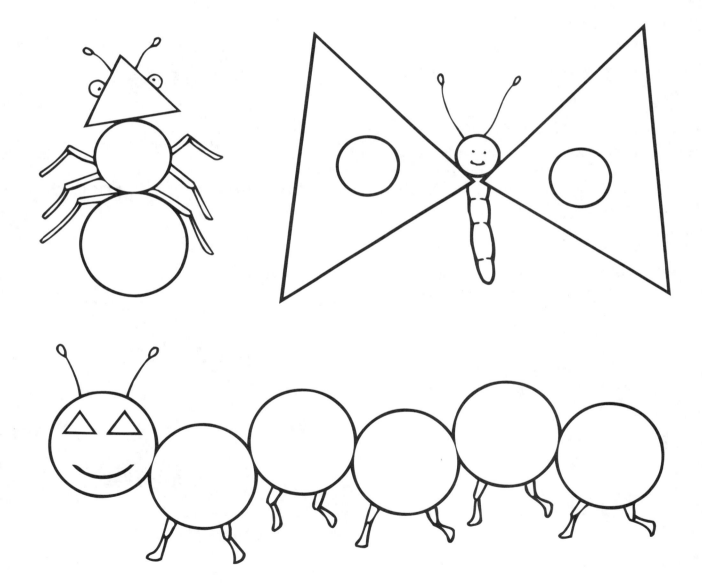

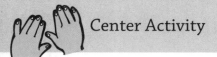

Working independently or in pairs, children match the two insects that are the same.

Make a Match

Creating the Center

1. Laminate and cut apart the cards on pages 79–83.
2. Place the cards in a sturdy envelope or folder.

Using the Center

1. Review the names of the insects shown on the cards.
2. Model how to match the cards. Explain to children that the color or size of the insect may be different, but the *type* of insect must be the same.
3. Children match all of the cards correctly.

Extension

Use these cards to play Concentration. Begin with six pairs of cards that match. Place the cards facedown in three rows of four. Players take turns turning over two cards. If the cards match, the player takes them. If not, the cards are turned back over. Play continues until all cards have been matched. Increase the number of cards being used as children gain more experience.

Materials

- pages 79–83, laminated
- scissors
- sturdy envelope or folder

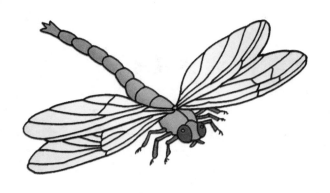

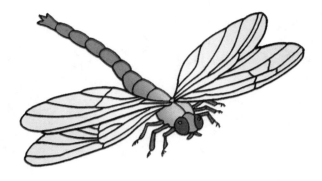

Make a Match

Make a Match

Make a Match

Make a Match

Make a Match

Make a Match

Make a Match

Make a Match

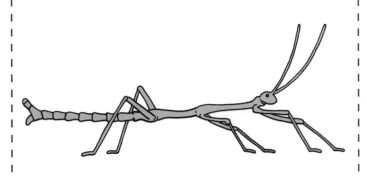
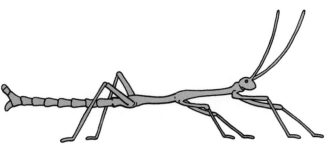

About Insects   **81**

Make a Match

Make a Match

Make a Match

Make a Match

Make a Match

Make a Match

Make a Match

Make a Match

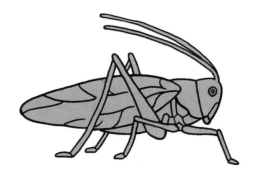
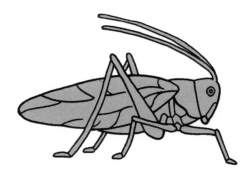

About Insects

Make a Match

Make a Match

Make a Match

Make a Match

Make a Match

Make a Match

Make a Match

Make a Match

Following the Insect

Children imitate the movement of various insects as they play this variation of Follow the Leader.

How to Play

1. Children form a line on the playground. They stand about an arm's length apart to allow for movement.

2. The leader says, *I am a* (insect name). *Follow me.* Then the leader starts off across the playground imitating the action of the named insect.

3. The other children follow along, performing the same action.

4. Once the leader has completed his or her turn, a new leader is chosen and play continues until each child has had a turn.

I am a bee. Follow me!

Children use insects on a stick as they name insects. Use the insects to present a quick little puppet show to classmates and parents.

Insect Play

Steps to Follow

1. Teach children the song "This Is the Way an Insect Moves" on page 87.

2. Tell children that they will be using the insects on craft sticks to share information with their classmates about how insects move.

3. Divide the children into four insect groups: grasshoppers, ants, ladybugs, and honeybees. Then have each group make their insect craft sticks.

4. Call up one group at a time. Each group sings its verse and acts out the movement being described.

Materials

- pages 88 and 89, reproduced, several copies of each insect

- craft sticks

- scissors

- tape

- glue

- crayons

Note: Sing this song to the tune of "The Mulberry Bush."

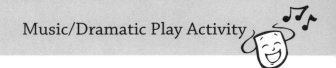

This Is the Way an Insect Moves

This is the way a grasshopper hops,
    a grasshopper hops,
    a grasshopper hops.
This is the way a grasshopper hops,
Early in the morning.

This is the way a honeybee flies,
    a honeybee flies,
    a honeybee flies.
This is the way a honeybee flies,
Early in the morning.

This is the way a red ant runs,
    a red ant runs,
    a red ant runs.
This is the way a red ant runs,
Early in the morning.

This is the way a ladybug walks,
    a ladybug walks,
    a ladybug walks.
This is the way a ladybug walks,
Early in the morning.

Note: Reproduce these patterns for Insect Play music/dramatic play activity.

Children color and cut out the pictures below and glue them to a craft stick. Then children use them to animate the song "This Is the Way an Insect Moves."

ant

ladybug

Note: Reproduce these patterns for Insect Play music/dramatic play activity.

Music/Dramatic Play Activity Pattern Pieces

Children color and cut out the pictures below and glue them to a craft stick. Then children use them to animate the song "This Is the Way an Insect Moves."

grasshopper

honeybee

3

Insect Life Cycles

Children are introduced to the life cycle of an insect.

Egg, Caterpillar, Butterfly

Pale yellow eggs hold a surprise.
One day they will be butterflies.

1

Hungry little caterpillar,
all you are doing is chewing,

2

chewing,

chewing.

Chrysalis of jade hanging on a stem,
hiding all the changes within.

5

Out comes a butterfly.

Flutter, flutter, fly.

Flutter, flutter, fly.
A gentle butterfly passes by.

8

The End

Egg, Caterpillar, Butterfly

Pale yellow eggs
hold a surprise.
One day they will
be butterflies.

1

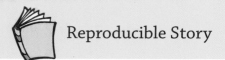
Note: Teachers will make copies and cut in half for minibooks.

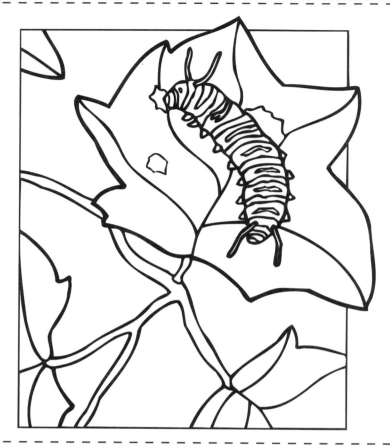

Hungry little
caterpillar,
all you are doing
is chewing,

2

chewing,

3

Note: Teachers will make copies and cut in half for minibooks.

Reproducible Story

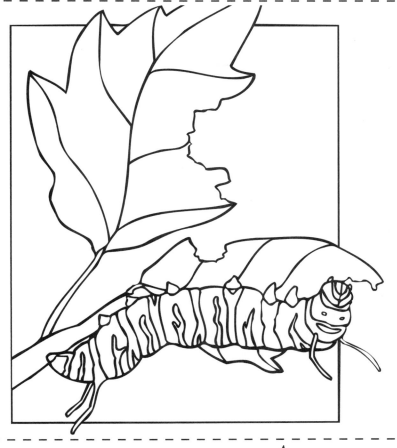

chewing.

4

Chrysalis of jade
hanging on a stem,
hiding all the
changes within.

5

Note: Teachers will make copies and cut in half for minibooks.

Out comes
a butterfly.

6

Flutter, flutter, fly.

7

Flutter, flutter, fly.
A gentle butterfly
passes by.

8

The End

Note: Children review the stages from egg to adult butterfly, then cut out and glue the steps in the correct order.

Name ____________________________

Color.

Cut.

Glue.

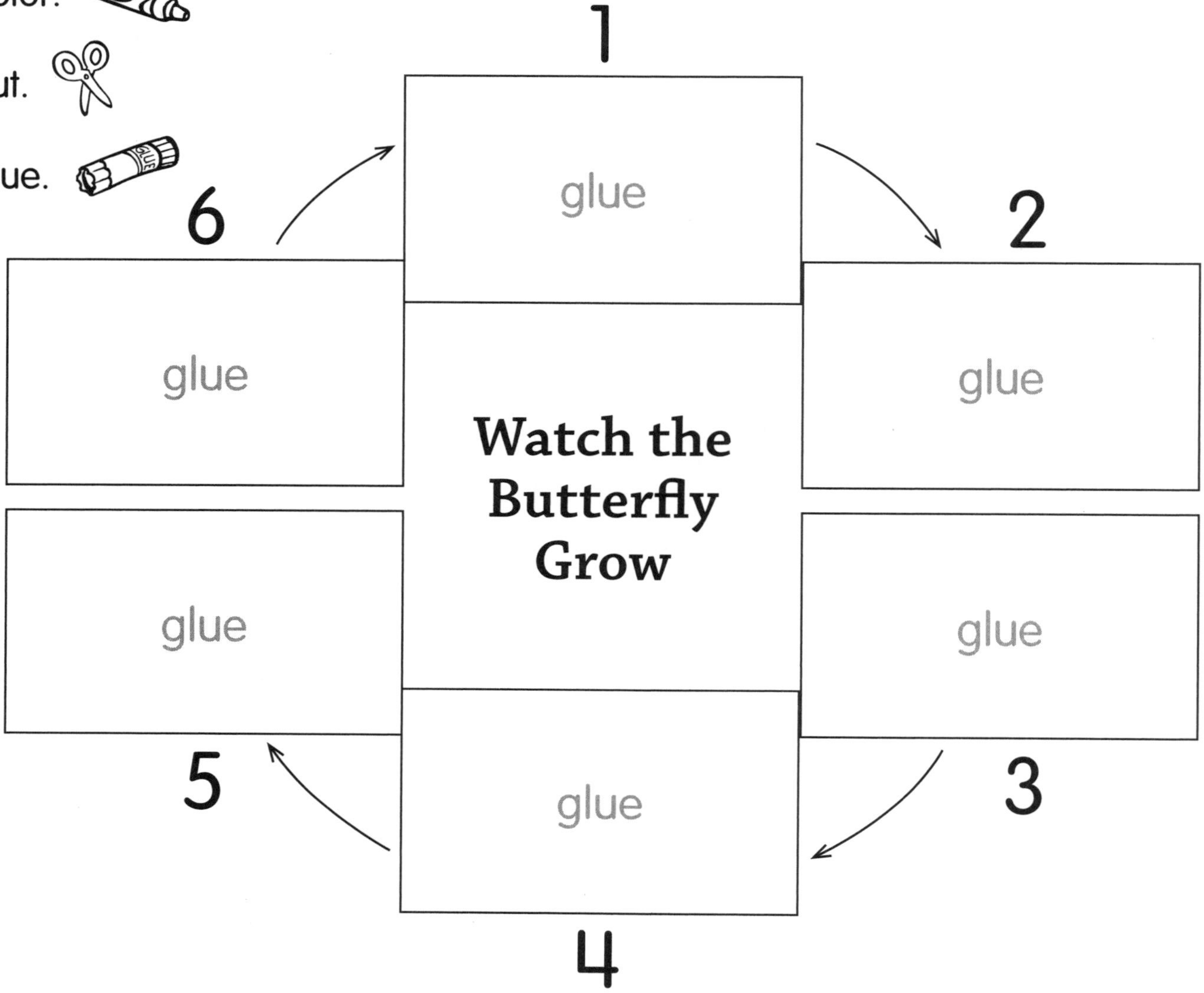
1
glue
2
glue
3
glue
4
glue
5
glue
6
glue
Watch the Butterfly Grow

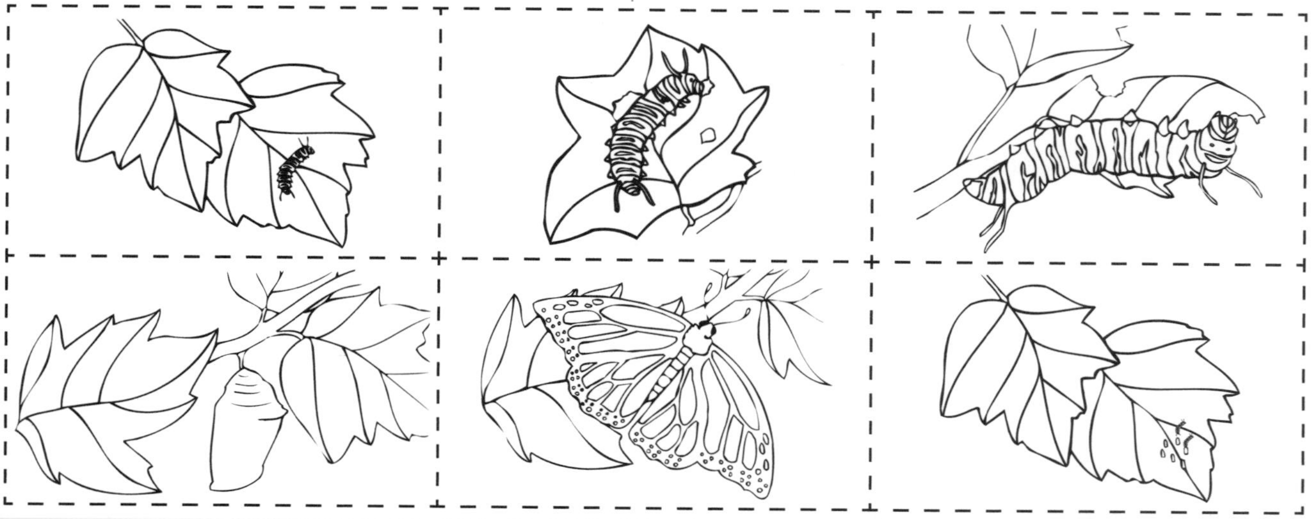

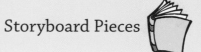
Note: See page 8 for suggestions on using the storyboard pieces on pages 107 and 109 for Egg, Caterpillar, Butterfly.

Insect Life Cycles

©2005 by Evan-Moor Corp.
All About Insects • EMC 2405

Insect Life Cycles

©2005 by Evan-Moor Corp.
All About Insects • EMC 2405

Insect Life Cycles

©2005 by Evan-Moor Corp.
All About Insects • EMC 2405

Insect Life Cycles **109**

Insect Life
Cycles

©2005 by Evan-Moor Corp.
All About Insects • EMC 2405

Insect Life Cycles

©2005 by Evan-Moor Corp.
All About Insects • EMC 2405

Insect Life Cycles

©2005 by Evan-Moor Corp.
All About Insects • EMC 2405

Children use stamp pads, their fingertips, and string to create lovely butterflies to "fly" around the room.

Materials

- page 112, reproduced, one per pair

- 9" x 12" (23 x 30.5 cm) colored construction paper, one sheet per child

- 3' (1 m) piece of string, one per child

- various colored stamp pads

- pipe cleaners, two per child

- crayons

- hole punch

- glue

- scissors

Spotted Butterfly on a String

Steps to Follow

1. Children work in pairs to trace the template onto sheets of colored construction paper. One child holds the template in place as the other traces the pattern. Then they switch.

2. They use crayons to color the butterfly's body.

3. Children use a stamp pad and their fingertips to make spots on the butterfly.

4. They cut out the butterfly.

5. Then they tape two pipe cleaners to the butterfly's head for antennae.

6. Assist children as needed with using the hole punch to punch a hole on the butterfly's head and tying a string through the hole.

7. Once butterflies are complete, hang the colorful, spotted butterflies around the classroom.

Extension

Children take their butterflies out to the playground and run around to make their butterflies "fly."

Note: Reproduce this pattern to use with Spotted Butterfly on a String art activity.

Butterfly Template

Yum! These butterfly sandwiches make a great afternoon snack. Children decide between a butter and jelly butterfly sandwich or a cream cheese and olive butterfly sandwich.

Butterfly Sandwiches

Materials

- sliced bread
- butter
- jelly (various colors)
- cream cheese
- sliced olives (black and green)
- thin pretzels
- plastic knives and spoons
- paper bowls and plates
- optional: milk, juice, paper cups

Preparation

1. Prepare a cooking center with all materials assembled.
2. Decide if children will work in small groups to make their sandwiches.
3. Trim crusts from bread slices and cut them in half diagonally.
4. Place sandwich ingredients in individual bowls (softened cream cheese, softened butter, pretzels, jelly, sliced olives). Place bread triangles on a plate.
5. Place knives, spoons, and paper plates at the table.

Steps to Follow

1. Children take two bread triangles and spread butter or cream cheese on the bread.
2. Next, children add spots of jelly or olive slices.
3. They place the bread on a plate to form butterfly wings.
4. Then children add two pretzel sticks for antennae.
5. They may enjoy the sandwiches with juice or milk.

Parent Letter

Dear Parent(s) or Guardian(s),

Today we cooked in class. Your child made "Butterfly Sandwiches." Besides having fun cooking and eating, the children practiced these skills:

- listening to and following directions
- vocabulary development
- using small motor skills

For our unit *Insects*, we will send home a variety of new recipes. Each recipe will be one that your child has tried in class and is excited about. We hope you have an opportunity to try this recipe again with your child. Allowing your child to help you in the kitchen is a wonderful way to reinforce learning skills while creating family memories.

Butterfly Sandwiches

Materials

- sliced bread
- butter
- jelly (various colors)
- cream cheese
- sliced olives (black and green)
- thin pretzels
- plastic knives and spoons
- bowls and plates
- milk or juice
- cups or glasses

Steps to Follow

1. Remove crusts from bread and cut the slices diagonally.
2. Take two bread triangles and spread them with butter or cream cheese.
3. Add spots of jelly or olive slices to decorate the wings.
4. Place the bread on a plate in the shape of butterfly wings.
5. Add two pretzel sticks for antennae.
6. Enjoy the sandwiches with juice or milk.

Note: Children say the name of each picture. Then they color the pictures whose names begin with the /c/ sound.

Name _____

Same Sound

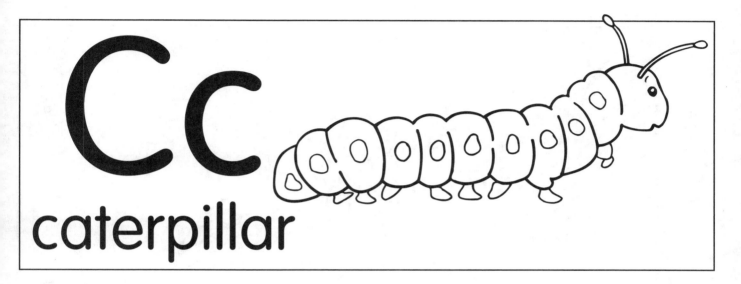

Color the pictures that begin like **caterpillar**.

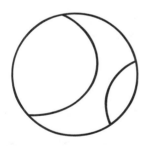

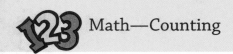

Note: Children count the number of each type of butterfly and record it.

Name _____

Butterflies

Count.

How many do you see?

 _____

 _____

 _____

Note: Review the numbers 1 to 20 and the shapes *circle, rectangle,* and *triangle.* Guide children to color the shapes in the color key. Children connect the dots and then color the butterfly's shapes.

Name _____

What Am I?

Connect the dots.
Color the shapes.

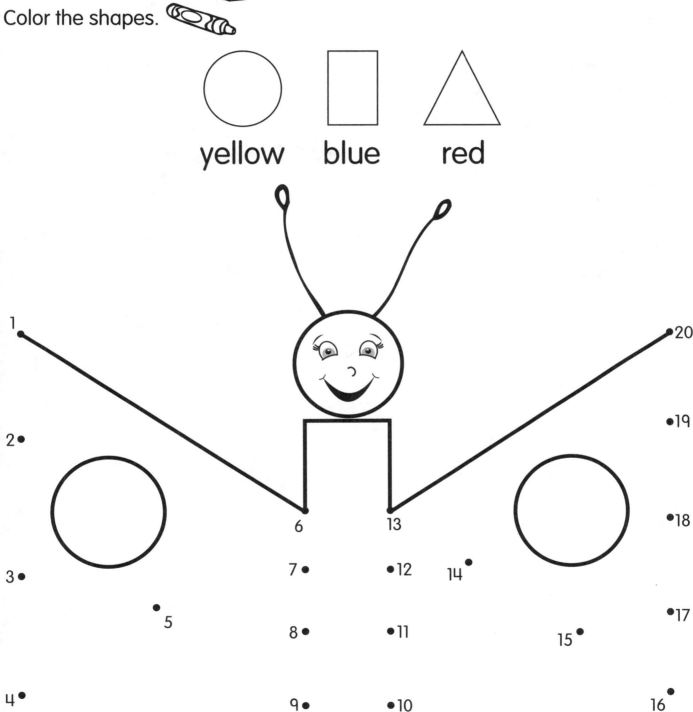

yellow   blue   red

Caterpillar

Creating the Center

1. Laminate the chart on page 119. Post it at the center.

2. Place all the materials needed at the center.

3. Cut apart the egg cartons to make 6-cup sections for the caterpillar.

4. Plan time to model how the center is used.

Using the Center

1. Individual or small groups of children may work at the center at one time.

2. Children take an egg carton section and color it, adding stripes or dots of color.

3. They add eyes and a mouth to one end of the section. Then children poke two toothpicks in the head for antennae.

Children recycle an egg carton to create a caterpillar.

Materials

- page 119, laminated
- egg cartons
- toothpicks (remove sharp points)
- scissors
- glue
- marking pens, crayons, or paint

Center Chart

1. Take an egg carton section.

2. Color the cups.

3. Add ⊙⊙ , ⌣ , and \\/ .

Relay Races

Preparation

1. Use long jump ropes to mark a starting line and a finish line.

2. Divide the class into several groups. Keep the groups small so children don't have to wait too long for a turn.

3. Plan to play in a large grassy space.

How to Play

1. The first child in each row pretends to be a caterpillar and crawls along the grass to the finish line. When the first child reaches the finish line, the next child in each row begins to crawl. Continue until all children have had a turn.

2. Next, the children pretend to be butterflies. The first child in each row flies back to the starting line with arms outstretched as wings. When the first child reaches the starting line, the next child in each row begins to "fly." Continue until all children have had a turn.

Take your little "caterpillars" and "butterflies" outdoors to a grassy area for this activity.

Materials

- two jump ropes

Fluttery Butterfly

A Finger Play

Fluttery butterfly,
(Join hands at thumbs and flap
hands to resemble wings.)

Yellow and black,

Sip at a flower
(Open one hand to resemble a flower.)

When you want a snack.
(Point forefinger into open hand.)

You spread your wings
(Form wings again.)

To rest in the sun,

And glide on the wind
(Make gliding motion.)

'Til the day is done.
(Fold hands and rest under cheek.)

Note: Reproduce these patterns to use as an alternative finger play for Fluttery Butterfly.

Children color, cut out, and tape the patterns to create finger puppets.

 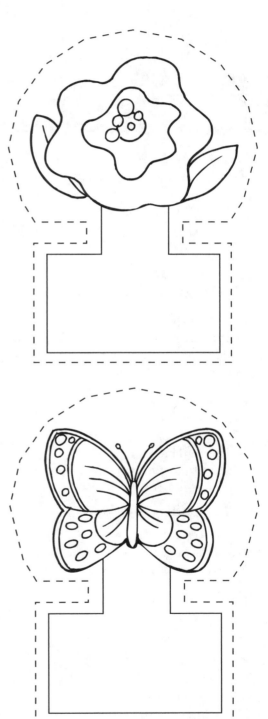

Insect Helpers

Children are presented with different ways in which insects help people and the environment.

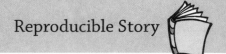

Good Bugs!

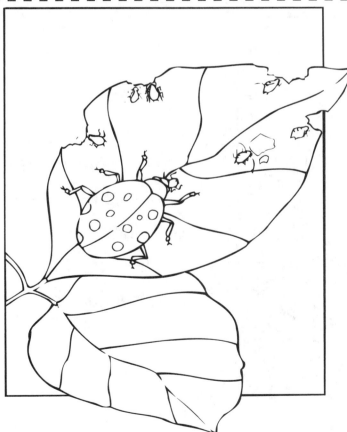

Hi!

I'm a helpful **ladybug**.

I eat little bugs

that eat plants.

But I am not the

only helpful insect.

1

Note: Teachers will make copies and cut in half for minibooks.

Hi!

I'm a helpful **lacewing**.

I eat little bugs that

eat plants, too.

But I am not the

only helpful insect.

2

Hi!

I'm a helpful **stinkbug**.

I eat little bugs that

eat plants, too.

But I am not the

only helpful insect.

3

Note: Teachers will make copies and cut in half for minibooks.

Reproducible Story

Hi!
I'm a helpful **mantis**.
I eat little bugs that
eat plants, too.
But I am not the
only helpful insect.

4

Hi!
I'm a helpful
silkworm moth.
My caterpillar makes
a cocoon of silk.
The silk is used to
make silk cloth.
But I am not the
only helpful insect.

5

Reproducible Story

Note: Teachers will make copies and cut in half for minibooks.

Hi!

I'm a helpful **honeybee**.

I move pollen from

flower to flower.

This helps make

new flowers.

6

We are all helpful insects.

7

Note: Teachers will make copies and cut in half for minibooks.

Reproducible Story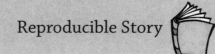

We are good bugs
that help plants
and people in
different ways.

8

The End

Note: After reviewing the story Good Bugs!, children find and color them.

Name _____

Is It a Good Bug?

Color 😊 yes if the picture shows a good bug.

Color ☹ no if the picture does <u>not</u> show a good bug.

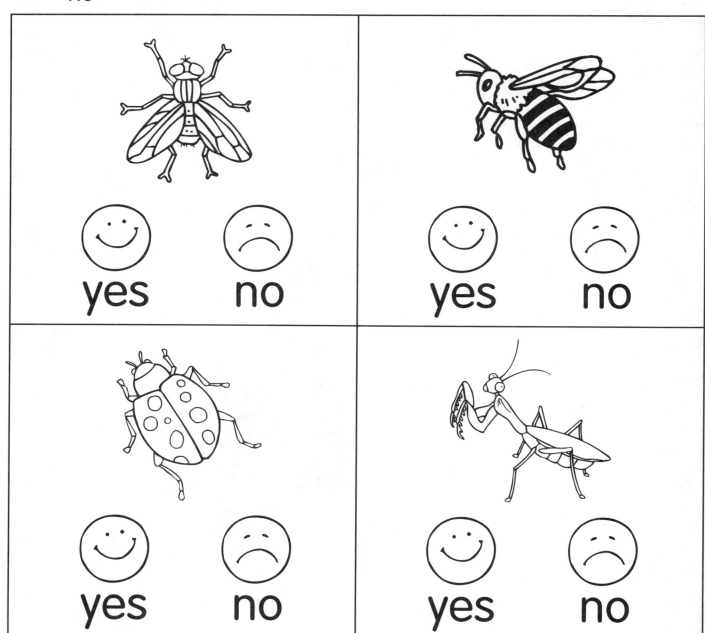

Note: See page 8 for suggestions on using the storyboard pieces on pages 141 and 143 for Good Bugs!

Storyboard Pieces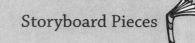

Insect
Helpers

Insect Helpers

Insect
Helpers

Insect Helpers

Insect Helpers

Insect
Helpers

Insect Helpers

Insect
Helpers

Insect Helpers

Insect Helpers

Insect
Helpers

Insect Helpers

Insect Helpers

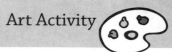
Children create busy worker bees flying around the hive.

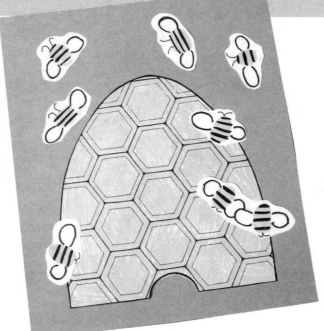

Materials

- page 146, reproduced, one per child
- blue construction paper, one per child
- white construction paper
- yellow tempera paint
- paper plates or pie pans
- thin black permanent markers
- newspaper or oilcloth table cover
- scissors
- wipes or paper towels for cleaning fingers

Busy Bees

Preparation

1. Cover a work area with newspaper or oilcloth.
2. Place a small amount of yellow paint in paper plates or pie pans.

Steps to Follow

1. Plan time to model how to make yellow fingerprint bee shapes on the white construction paper. Follow the example below. (**A**, **B**, **C**)
2. Children color and cut out the beehive on page 146.
3. Children glue the beehive to the blue construction paper.
4. Children dip their thumb into the yellow paint and make several thumbprints on the white construction paper. Allow time for the thumbprints to dry.
5. Children use a black marker to add black lines, wings, and antennae to their bees. Then they cut out and glue their bees around the hive.

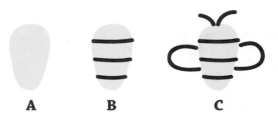

A   **B**   **C**

Art Activity Pattern Piece

Note: Reproduce this pattern to use with Busy Bees art activity.

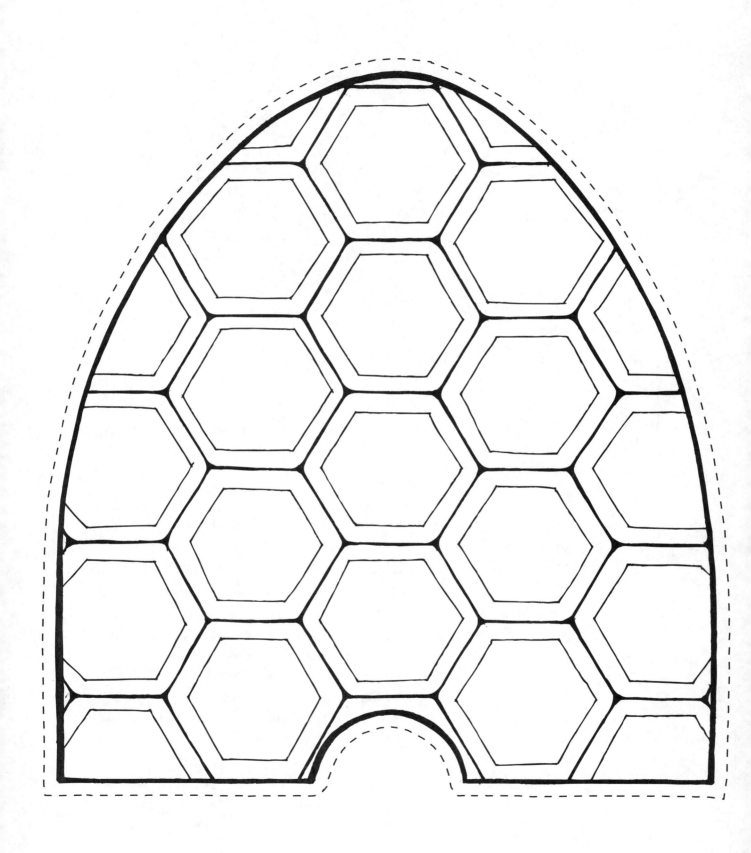

Note: Check for allergies before beginning any cooking activity.
An allergic reaction can occur through taste, smell, or contact with allergens.

Cooking Activity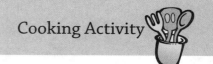

Provide a jar of honey containing a honeycomb for children to examine. (A magnifying glass helps them take a closer look at the shape of a cell.) End the lesson with honey on crackers.

Materials

- honey with a honeycomb
- crackers
- small paper plates
- dull plastic knives
- optional: magnifying glass

A Taste of Honey

Steps to Follow

1. Share the honeycomb with children. (Provide time for small groups to take a closer look.) Ask children to describe the honeycomb. Discuss the number of sides in each honeycomb cell. Explain that bees make the honey.

2. Small groups of children go to the honey center to spread honey on crackers for a snack.

3. While you all enjoy your honey and crackers, ask children to tell about other things they eat that contain honey.

Dear Parent(s) or Guardian(s),

Today we prepared a snack called "A Taste of Honey." The children also learned about honeycombs. Besides having fun cooking and eating, the children practiced these skills:

- listening to and following directions
- vocabulary development
- using small motor skills

For our unit *Insects*, we will send home a variety of new recipes. Each recipe will be one that your child has tried in class and is excited about. We hope you have an opportunity to try this recipe again with your child. Allowing your child to help you in the kitchen is a wonderful way to reinforce learning skills while creating family memories.

A Taste of Honey

Materials

- honey
- crackers
- plastic knife
- paper plate

Steps to Follow

1. Take a cracker.
2. Use the knife to get a bit of honey from the jar.
3. Spread honey on the cracker.
4. Enjoy!

Note: After naming all of the pictures on the page, children color the pictures that rhyme with *tree*.

Language—Rhyming Words

Name _____

Rhymes with Tree

Color the pictures that rhyme with **tree**.

Note: Children cut out and glue the letter that makes the beginning sound of each word.

Name _____

Bee  Begins with "B"

Cut ✂ and glue 🖊 the missing letter.

glue	**ree**

glue	**ee**

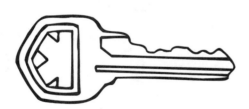

glue	**ey**

t   b   k

All About Insects • EMC 2405 • ©2005 by Evan-Moor Corp.

Note: Sing this song to the tune of "Ten Little Indians" with children. Then they write the numbers 1 through 10 under the bees.

Math—Counting

Name _____

Ten Little Honeybees

1 little, 2 little, 3 little honeybees
4 little, 5 little, 6 little honeybees
7 little, 8 little, 9 little honeybees
10 little honeybees go buzz.

Count the honeybees.

1   2

___ ___ ___ ___ ___

___ ___ ___ ___ ___

Working in pairs, children count and match insects to play a simple game of dominoes.

Good Bug Dominoes

Creating the Center

1. Laminate and cut apart pages 153 and 155.
2. Store the cards in a sturdy folder or envelope.
3. Plan time to model how the center is used.

Using the Center

1. Children play in pairs.
2. They turn all of the dominoes facedown and mix them up.
3. One child picks one domino and sets it faceup in the middle of the table.
4. Each player then takes four dominoes and holds them in his or her hand, making sure the other player cannot see them.
5. The first player tries to match one of his or her dominoes to the one in the middle of the table. If a match is made, play moves to the other player. If a match cannot be made, the player takes a new domino. If a match still cannot be made, play moves to the other player.
6. Play continues until all of the dominoes have been picked up. The player with the fewest (or no) dominoes left is the winner.

Materials

- pages 153 and 155, laminated
- sturdy folder or envelope

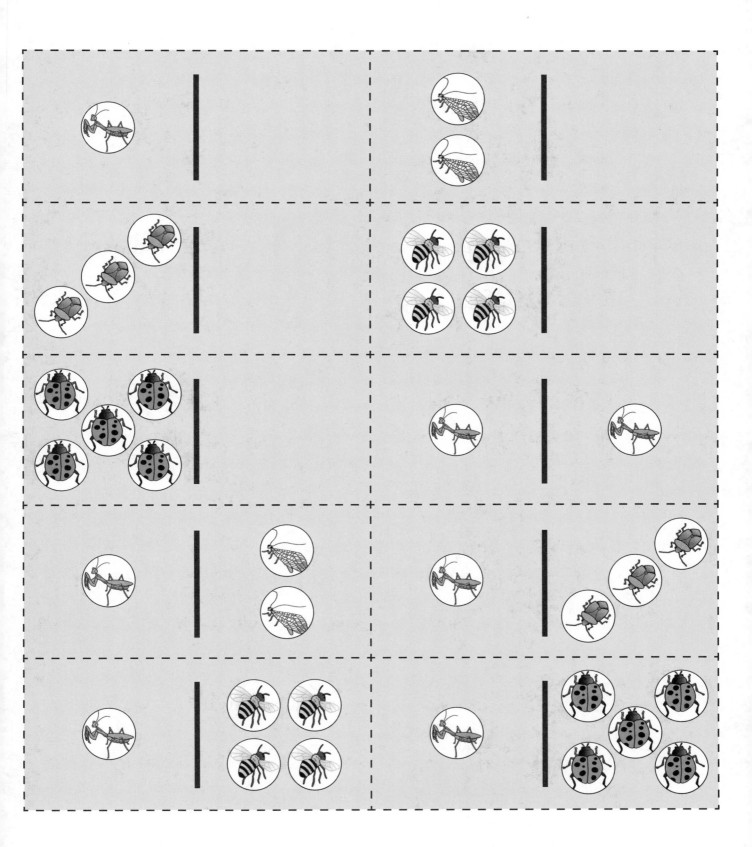

Good Bug Dominoes

Good Bug Dominoes

Good Bug Dominoes

Good Bug Dominoes

Good Bug Dominoes

Good Bug Dominoes

Good Bug Dominoes

Good Bug Dominoes

Good Bug Dominoes

Good Bug Dominoes

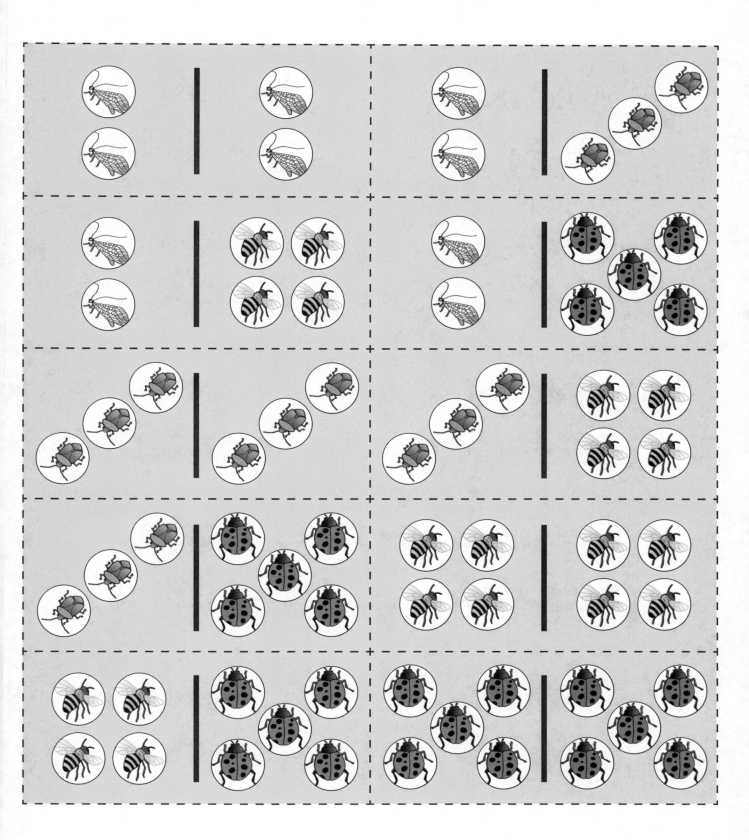

Good Bug Dominoes

©2005 by Evan-Moor Corp.
All About Insects • EMC 2405

Good Bug Dominoes

©2005 by Evan-Moor Corp.
All About Insects • EMC 2405

Good Bug Dominoes

©2005 by Evan-Moor Corp.
All About Insects • EMC 2405

Good Bug Dominoes

©2005 by Evan-Moor Corp.
All About Insects • EMC 2405

Good Bug Dominoes

©2005 by Evan-Moor Corp.
All About Insects • EMC 2405

Good Bug Dominoes

©2005 by Evan-Moor Corp.
All About Insects • EMC 2405

Good Bug Dominoes

©2005 by Evan-Moor Corp.
All About Insects • EMC 2405

Good Bug Dominoes

©2005 by Evan-Moor Corp.
All About Insects • EMC 2405

Good Bug Dominoes

©2005 by Evan-Moor Corp.
All About Insects • EMC 2405

Good Bug Dominoes

©2005 by Evan-Moor Corp.
All About Insects • EMC 2405

Flower, Flower, Honeybee

Flower, Flower, Honeybee is played like the game Duck, Duck, Goose.

How to Play

1. Children sit cross-legged in a circle facing each other.

2. Select a child to be "It."

3. The child who is It walks around the outside of the circle, gently tapping each person on the head and calling him or her "Flower."

4. As soon as the child who is It taps a child and calls him or her "Honeybee," the Honeybee gets up and chases It around the circle.

5. It tries to sit in the Honeybee's spot before being tagged.

6. If the Honeybee tags It before he or she is safely in the Honeybee's spot, It must sit in the middle of the circle, and the Honeybee becomes It for the next round.

7. The player in the center must remain there until another player is tagged.

Where Are the Bees?

A Finger Play

Here is the beehive.
Where are the bees?
Hiding away where
nobody sees.

They are coming out now.
They are all alive.
One!

Two!

Three!

Four!

Five!

Extension

Use the patterns on page 159 to make finger puppets to
accompany this finger play.

Note: Reproduce these patterns to use as an alternative finger play for Where Are the Bees?

 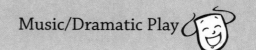
Children color, cut out, and tape to make these bee finger puppets.

A Spider Is Not an Insect!

Children learn to distinguish
between a spider and an insect.

Note: Teachers will make copies
and cut in half for minibooks.

Reproducible Story

What Is It?

"Wow! Look at
that big bug!"
said Anna.

1

Reproducible Story

Note: Teachers will make copies and cut in half for minibooks.

"It's not a bug,"
said Father.

"What is it?"
asked Anna.

2

"A bug has six
legs," said Father.

"How many legs
do you see?"

3

"I see eight legs,"
answered Anna.

4

"A spider has eight
legs," said Father.
"That is a spider."

5

Note: Teachers will make copies and cut in half for minibooks.

Anna watched the spider spin a web.

"Why is the spider making a web?" asked Anna.

6

"This spider catches insects in the sticky web," answered Father.

"The spider will eat the insects it catches."

7

Note: Teachers will make copies and cut in half for minibooks.

Reproducible Story

"Wow! Look at that big spider!" said Anna.

8

The End

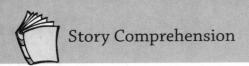

Story Comprehension

Note: Children count the number of legs on each creature, write the number, then circle *insect* or *spider*.

Name _____

Insect or Spider?

insect   spider

6 legs   8 legs

Count. Write. Circle.

I see ___ legs.  insect spider	I see ___ legs.  insect spider
I see ___ legs.  insect spider	I see ___ legs. 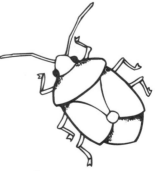 insect spider

Note: See page 9 for suggestions on using the storyboard pieces on pages 177 and 179 for What Is It?

Storyboard Pieces

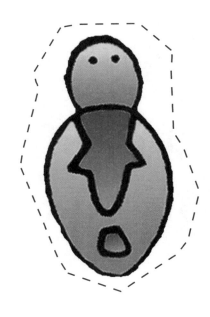

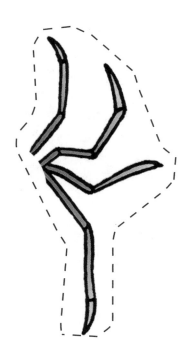

spider

insect

A Spider Is
Not an Insect!

A Spider Is
Not an Insect!

A Spider Is
Not an Insect!

A Spider Is Not an Insect!

A Spider Is
Not an Insect!

A Spider Is
Not an Insect!

A Spider Is
Not an Insect!

A Spider Is Not an Insect!

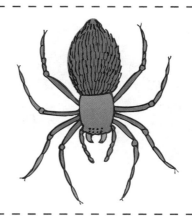

A Spider Is Not an Insect!

©2005 by Evan-Moor Corp.
All About Insects • EMC 2405

A Spider Is Not an Insect!

©2005 by Evan-Moor Corp.
All About Insects • EMC 2405

A Spider Is Not an Insect!

©2005 by Evan-Moor Corp.
All About Insects • EMC 2405

A Spider Is Not an Insect!

©2005 by Evan-Moor Corp.
All About Insects • EMC 2405

A Spider Is Not an Insect!

©2005 by Evan-Moor Corp.
All About Insects • EMC 2405

A Spider Is Not an Insect!

©2005 by Evan-Moor Corp.
All About Insects • EMC 2405

A Spider Is Not an Insect!

©2005 by Evan-Moor Corp.
All About Insects • EMC 2405

A Spider Is Not an Insect!

©2005 by Evan-Moor Corp.
All About Insects • EMC 2405

Note: Review the number of legs on a spider (8) and introduce the fact that many spiders have 8 eyes.

Art Activity

Children review spider facts as they make really big spiders.

Materials

- 4" x 12" (10 x 30.5 cm) black construction paper, one per child

- 1" x 9" (2.5 x 23 cm) strips of black construction paper, eight per child

- 4" square (10 cm) black construction paper, one per child

- colorful peel-and-stick dots, eight per child

- glue

- piece of white or yellow chalk

- tape

Spiders

One leg, two legs,
three legs, four!
You mean to tell me
you have more?

Five legs, six legs,
seven legs, eight!
I think spiders are really great!

Spider Headbands

Preparation

1. Prepare an art center with all materials assembled.
2. Cut construction paper to size.
3. Fold the larger black construction paper strips in half.
4. Count out sets of eight peel-and-stick dots.
5. Plan time to model the steps for this project.

Steps to Follow

1. Give each child a set of materials.
2. Children round the corners of the black square to create a circle. (An adult may need to do this for younger students.)
3. Then they attach eight dots to the spider's head.
4. Children draw a mouth using white or yellow chalk.
5. They glue one folded strip of black paper to each side of the spider's head.
6. Children fold the "legs" back and forth accordion-style.
7. Then they glue four legs to each side of the head on the headband.
8. Once the glue dries, an adult places the headband around the child's head and fits it to size. The adult then tapes the headband together.

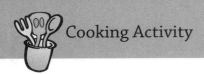 Cooking Activity

Note: Check for allergies before beginning any cooking activity. An allergic reaction can occur through taste, smell, or contact with allergens.

Spider Snacks

Preparation

1. Prepare a cooking center with all materials assembled.

2. Set up a work area covered with a plastic tablecloth to make cleanup easier. Have paper towels and hand wipes handy.

3. Plan time to model the steps for this cooking activity.

Steps to Follow

1. Children count out eight strips of licorice.

2. Then they push four licorice strips into the frosting on each side of the cookie to form legs.

3. Children squeeze out eight little eyes on the top of the cookie.

4. Once all of the cookie spiders are complete, enjoy a tasty snack.

Extension

As children eat their spider cookies, review the number of legs that a spider has and how it differs from the number of legs that an insect has.

Eat a spider? Yuck! These "spiders" are different—children love to munch on these tasty spiders.

Materials

• black sandwich cookies (Oreo®, for example)

• white frosting in squeeze tubes (for eyes)

• black licorice strings, eight per child

• paper towels

• hand wipes

• plastic tablecloth

Dear Parent(s) or Guardian(s),

Today we cooked in class. Your child made "Spider Snacks." Besides having fun cooking and eating, the children practiced these skills:

- listening to and following directions
- vocabulary development
- counting
- using small motor skills

For our unit *Insects*, we will send home a variety of new recipes. Each recipe will be one that your child has tried in class and is excited about. We hope you have an opportunity to try this recipe again with your child. Allowing your child to help you in the kitchen is a wonderful way to reinforce learning skills while creating family memories.

Spider Snacks

Materials

- black sandwich cookies (Oreo®, for example)
- white frosting in squeeze tubes (for eyes)
- black licorice strings
- paper towels

Steps to Follow

1. Count out eight strips of licorice.
2. Next, push four pieces of licorice into the frosting on each side of the cookie to form legs.
3. Have your child squeeze out eight little eyes on the top of the cookie.
4. Once all of the cookie spiders have been completed, enjoy a tasty snack.

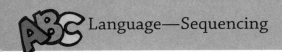
Note: After singing "Itsy-Bitsy Spider," children cut out and glue the pictures in the correct order.

Name _____

Itsy-Bitsy Spider

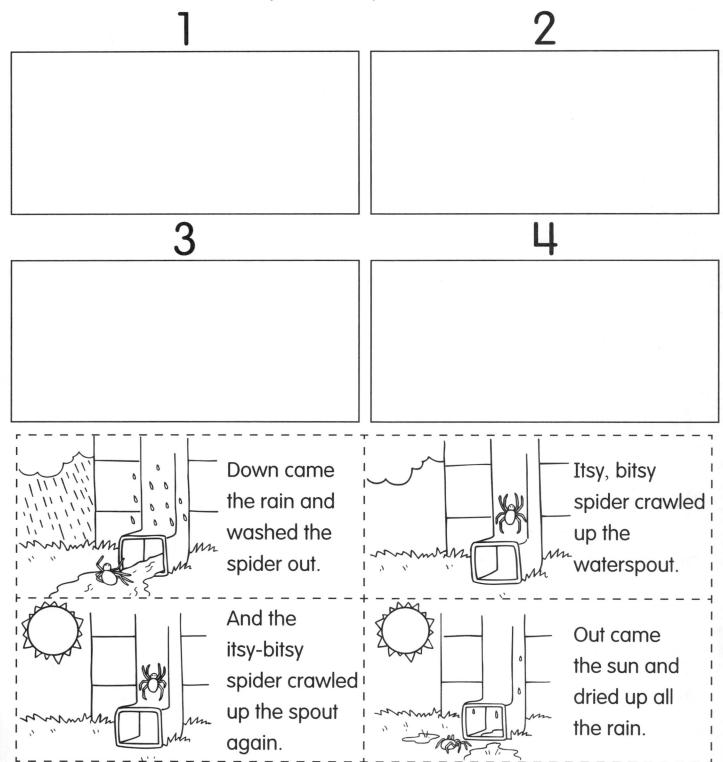

1

2

3

4

Down came the rain and washed the spider out.

Itsy, bitsy spider crawled up the waterspout.

And the itsy-bitsy spider crawled up the spout again.

Out came the sun and dried up all the rain.

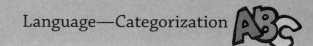

Note: Review the color words with children. Children trace a line from the bee to its hive and from the spider to its web.

Name _____

Find Their Home

Trace.

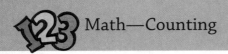
Note: After connecting the dots to complete the spider, children count and write the number of legs.

Name _____

Spider Legs

1 2 3 4 5 6 7 8 9 10 11 12 13 14 15 16 17 18 19 20

Connect the dots. Count.

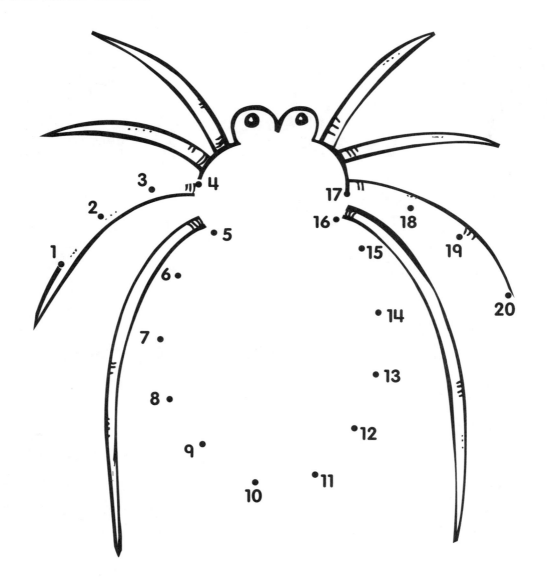

I see _____ spider legs.

Children collect flies for Spider's lunch by tossing two beanbags at flies on the spider web chart.

Materials

- page 188, reproduced
- page 189, reproduced, one per child
- large sheet of posterboard
- marking pens
- two beanbags
- scissors
- masking tape
- pencil

Flies for Lunch

Creating the Center

1. Make a spider web chart by drawing a giant spider web on the posterboard.
2. Cut apart the fly pictures on page 188 and glue them to the chart in various positions.
3. Tape the chart to the floor and use a strip of masking tape to mark the throwing line.
4. Place a supply of answer forms, a pencil, and a beanbag on a table.
5. Plan time to model how to use the center.

Using the Center

1. Children write their name on the "Spider's Lunch" answer form (page 189).
2. Children try to toss a spider beanbag onto a fly picture. Then they use the answer form to circle the number of flies their beanbag landed on.
3. They toss a second beanbag and again circle the number of flies their beanbag landed on.
4. Children repeat the steps above until they have tossed the beanbag four times.

How to Make a Beanbag

Cut two 5" (13 cm) circles from felt. Stitch the circles together, leaving an opening for filling. Fill with beans or rice, then stitch closed. You may wish to sew on eight "spider legs."

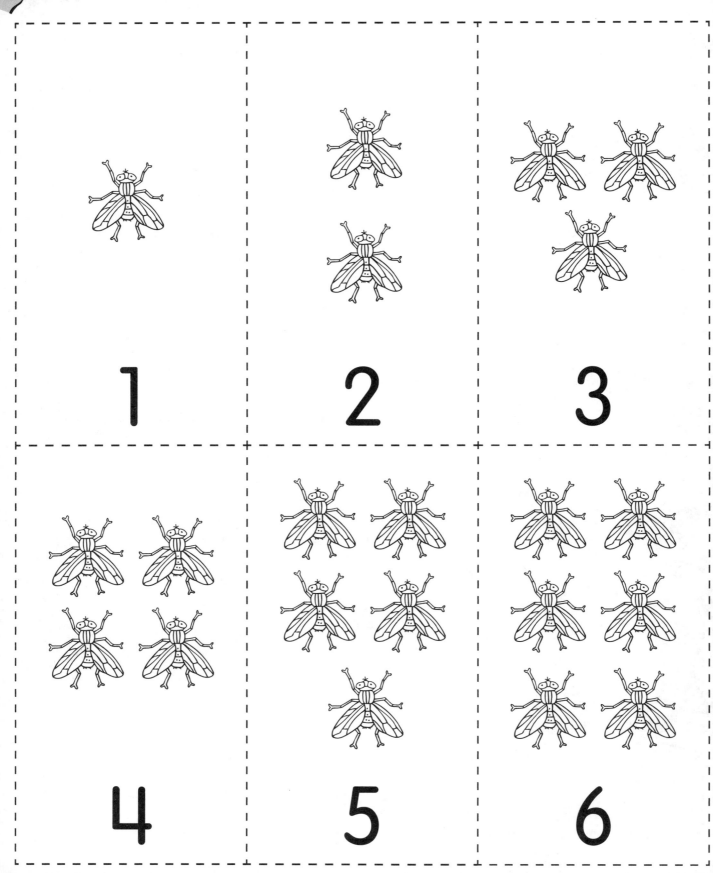

1

2

3

4

5

6

Note: Use this answer form for Flies for Lunch center activity.

Center Activity—Answer Form

Name _____

Spider's Lunch

Circle the number of flies your beanbag landed on.

Toss 1

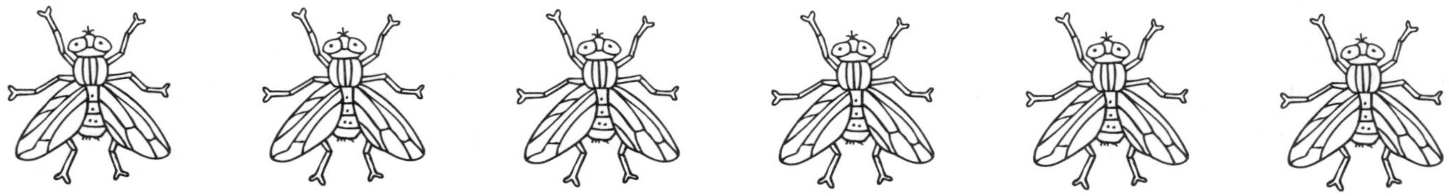

Toss 2

Toss 3

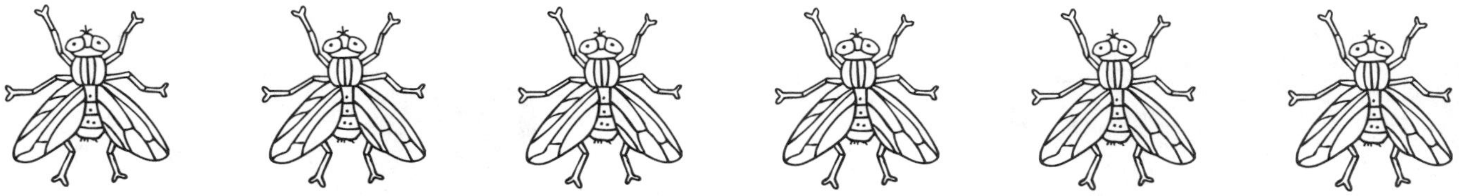

Toss 4

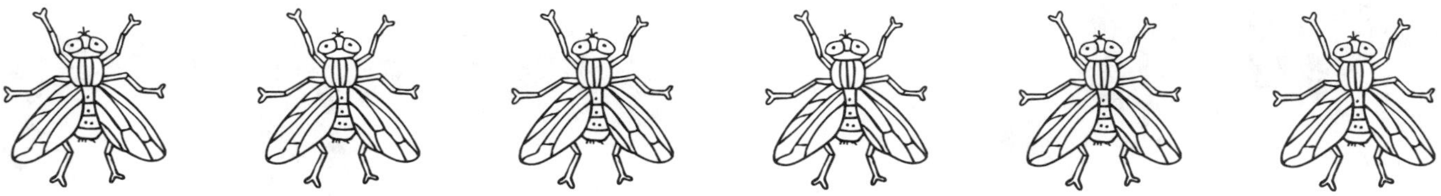

How many in all?

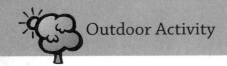

"Catch the Fly" Tag

Take your little "flies" and "spiders" outdoors to play this game of tag.

Preparation

Choose an outdoor area where you can define a play space. You may wish to use chalk to draw a border to limit the space in which children can run.

How to Play

1. Select one child to be the hungry "spider." The spider wears a spider headband (see page 181) to identify himself or herself.

2. The rest of the children are "flies."

3. At your signal, the spider begins to chase the flies. All the flies try to run away from the spider.

4. When the spider catches (tags) a fly, they change roles and the new spider tries to catch another fly.

Variation

If you have a large class, you may choose to have two or three spiders at one time.

Note: This activity includes the use of the spider headband on page 181.

Music/Dramatic Play Activity

Using a few simple props, children dramatize this old familiar nursery rhyme.

Materials

- small stool for tuffet
- plastic bowl and spoon
- spider headband (see page 181)

Little Miss Muffet

Preparation

Have the whole class practice reciting "Little Miss Muffet."

Steps to Follow

1. Select a child to portray Miss Muffet and a child to portray the spider.

2. Have Miss Muffet sit on the tuffet with her bowl and spoon.

3. Have the spider wear the spider headband (page 181).

4. Have the class recite the verse as Miss Muffet eats her curds and whey until the spider creeps up and frightens her away.

5. Repeat the drama several times with a new pair of actors each time.

Extension

Bring in cottage cheese, bowls, and spoons so the class can experience "curds and whey" (the lumpy part and the liquid part).

Alphabet Cards

Use these colorful Alphabet Cards in a variety of ways. Simply laminate and cut apart the cards and store them in a sturdy envelope or box.

Alphabet cards can be used to practice skills such as:

- letter recognition
- letter-sound association
- visual perception

Alphabet Card Games

What's My Name?	Use the alphabet cards to introduce the names of the letters, both uppercase and lowercase.
Make a Match	Children match a lowercase and uppercase letter. They then turn the cards over to self-check. If a correct match has been made, the child will see a picture of the same object whose name begins with the letter being matched.
First-Sound Game	Use the alphabet cards as phonics flash cards and ask children to identify the sound of each letter.
ABC Order	Children take all of the uppercase or lowercase cards and place them in alphabetical order.

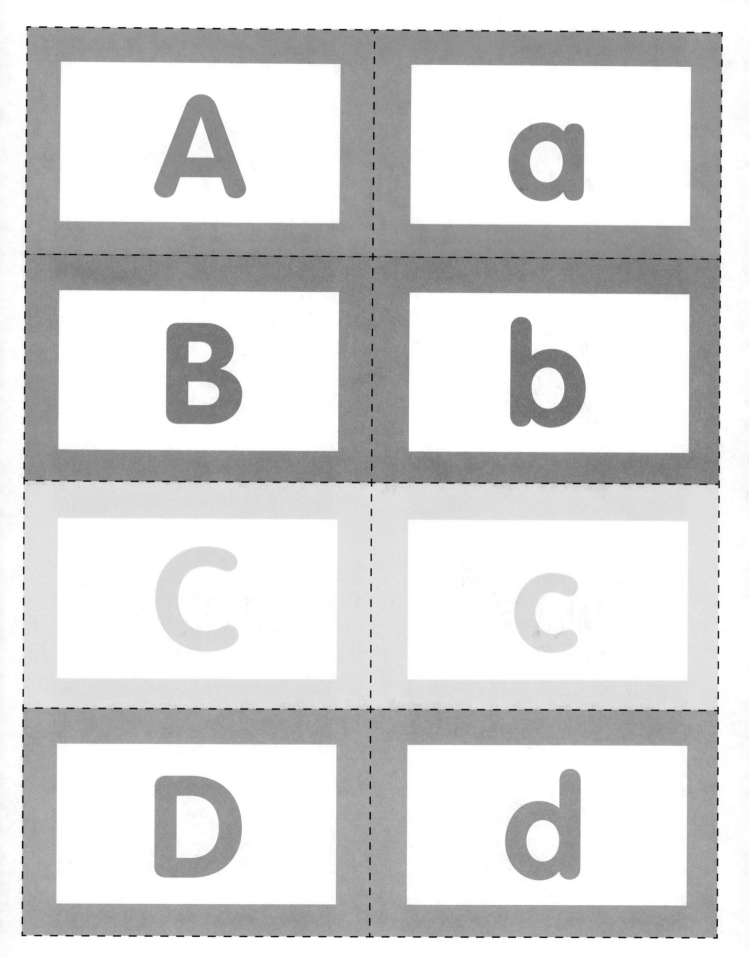

ant

©2005 by Evan-Moor Corp. • All About Insects • EMC 2405

Ant

©2005 by Evan-Moor Corp. • All About Insects • EMC 2405

butterfly

©2005 by Evan-Moor Corp. • All About Insects • EMC 2405

Butterfly

©2005 by Evan-Moor Corp. • All About Insects • EMC 2405

caterpillar

©2005 by Evan-Moor Corp. • All About Insects • EMC 2405

Caterpillar

©2005 by Evan-Moor Corp. • All About Insects • EMC 2405

dog

©2005 by Evan-Moor Corp. • All About Insects • EMC 2405

Dog

©2005 by Evan-Moor Corp. • All About Insects • EMC 2405

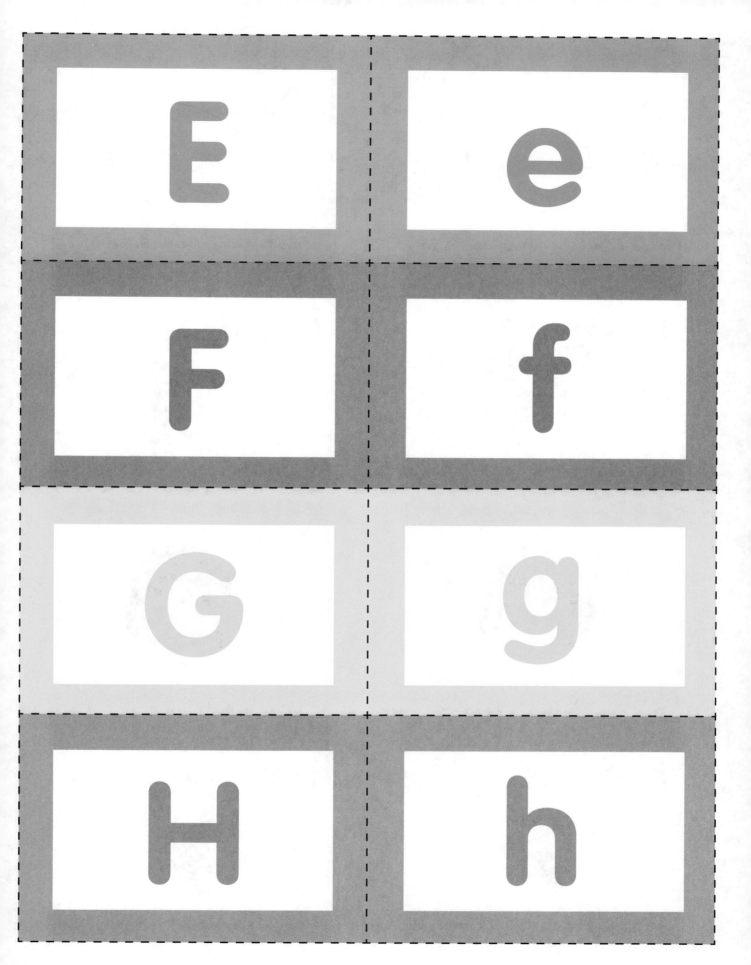

egg

Egg
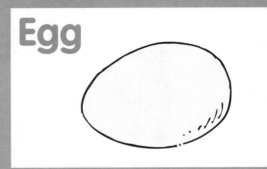

finger
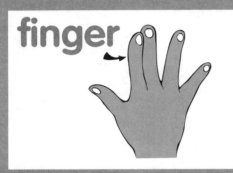

Finger
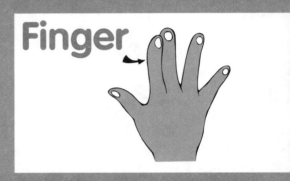

girl

Girl

honeybee

Honeybee

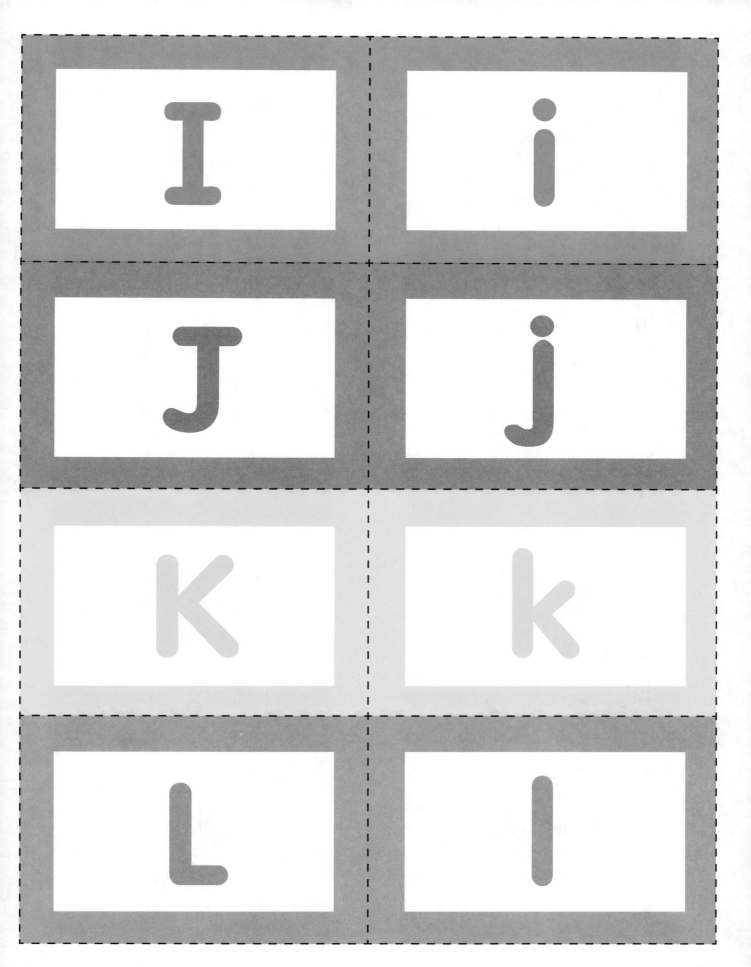

insects

Insects

jar

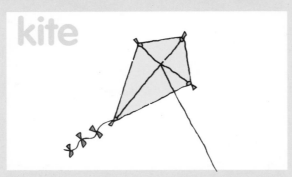

Jar

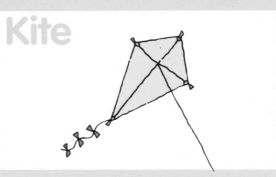

kite

Kite

ladybug

Ladybug

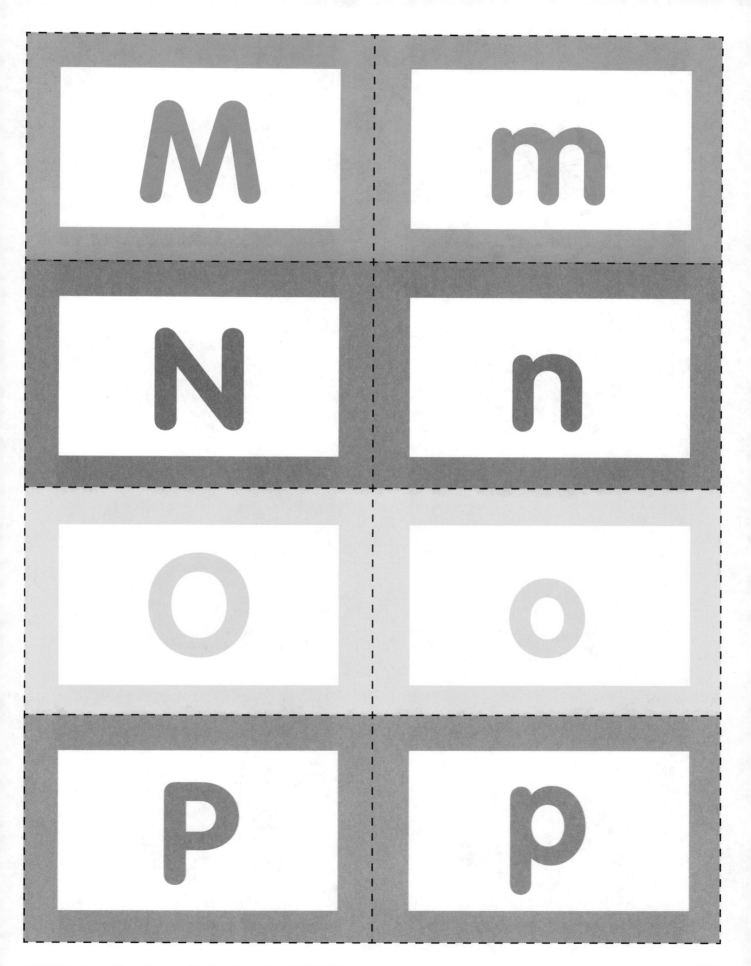

mouse

Mouse

nest

Nest

on/off

On/Off

pond

Pond

queen bee

Queen bee

red ball

Red ball

sun

Sun

turtle

Turtle

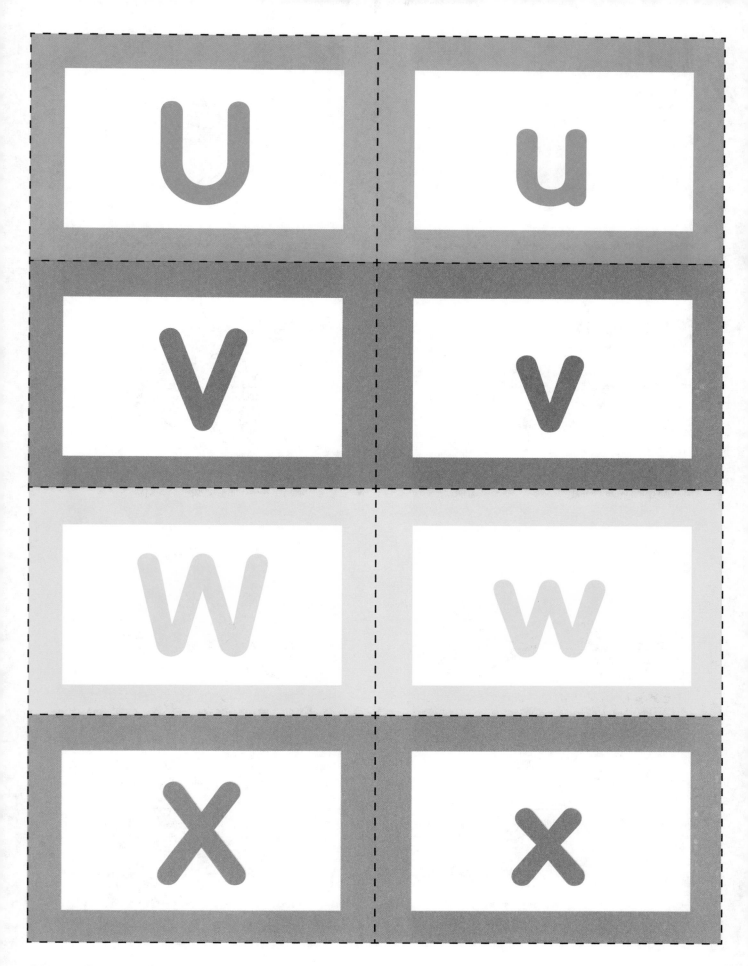

up

Up

vegetable

Vegetable

walking stick

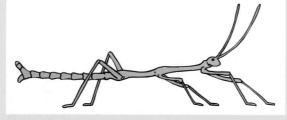

Walking stick

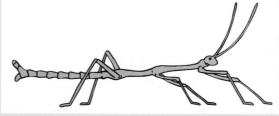

x-ray

X-ray

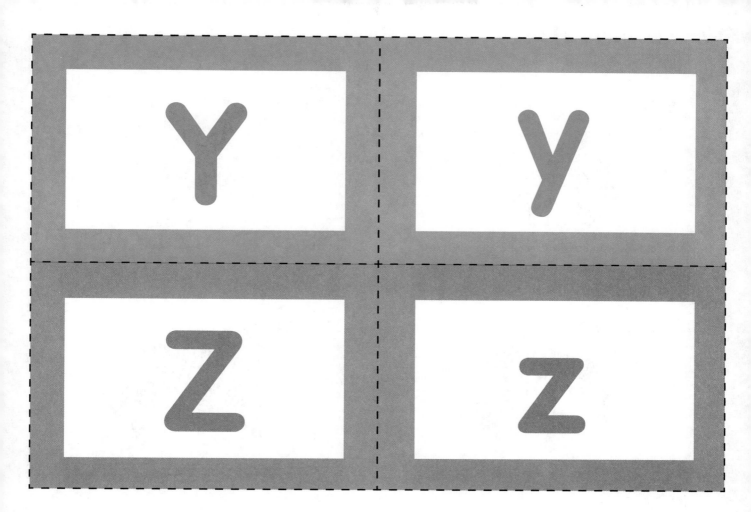

yellow jacket

Yellow jacket

zebra

Zebra

Answer Key

Page 28

Page 36

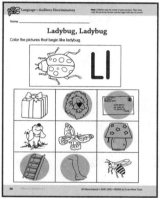

Page 37

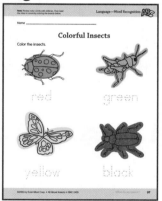

Page 38

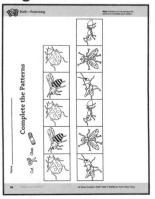

Page 39

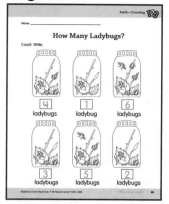

Page 66

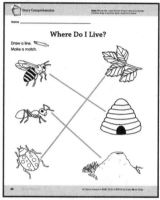

Page 74

Page 75

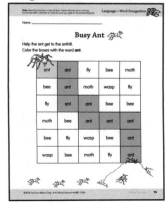

Page 76

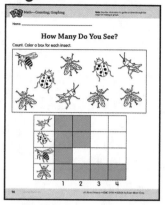

Page 77

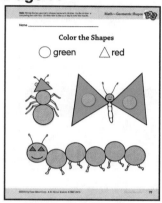

Page 106

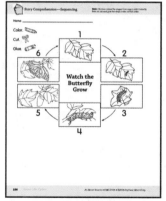

Page 115

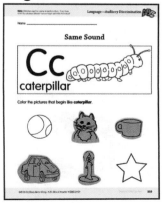

Page 116

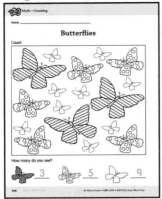

Page 117

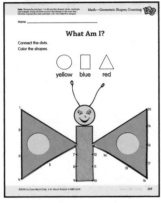

Page 140

Page 149

Page 150

Page 151

Page 176

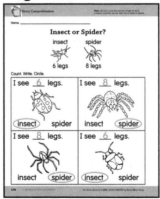

Page 184

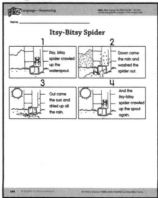

Page 185

Page 186

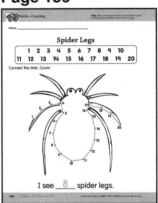

All About Insects • EMC 2405 • ©2005 by Evan-Moor Corp.